Serial Killer Trivia

500 Insomnia-inducing True Crime Facts and Details to Keep You Up All Night

True Crime Fanatics Volume 1

Nancy Alyssa Veysey, Kurtis-Giles Veysey, and True Crime Seven

TRUE CRIME Z

ISBN: 9798560436452

Table of Contents

Explore the Stories of

The Murderous Minds

A Note

From True Crime Seven

Hi there!

Thank you so much for picking up our book! Before you continue your exploration into the dark world of killers, we wanted to take a quick moment to explain the purpose of our books.

Our goal is to simply explore and tell the stories of various killers in the world: from unknown murderers to infamous serial killers. Our books are designed to be short and inclusive; we want to tell a good scary true story that anyone can enjoy regardless of their reading level.

That is why you won't see too many fancy words or complicated sentence structures in our books. Also, to prevent the typical cut and dry style of true crime books, we try to keep the narrative easy to follow while incorporating fiction style storytelling. As to information, we often find ourselves with too little or too much. So, in terms of research material and content, we always try to include what further helps the story of the killer.

Lastly, we want to acknowledge that, much like history, true crime is a subject that can often be interpreted differently. Depending on the topic and your upbringing, you might agree or disagree with how we present a story. We understand disagreements are inevitable. That is why we added this note, so hopefully, it can help you better understand our position and goal.

Now without further ado, let the exploration to the dark begin!

Introduction

THE GENRE OF TRUE CRIME HAS BECOME extremely popular. There are so many reasons for this interest. This book alone could not possibly provide space to name them all.

Idle curiosity, such as that causing people to slow down and rubberneck at the sight of a traffic accident, is one. A desire to understand the motive behind violent attacks, with an eye toward preventing future similar crimes, is yet another.

Whatever your reason for picking up this book in particular, we hope you will find something here you have never heard before. We started out with the idea of a writing a serial killer trivia book, and as it evolved, we added more categories.

As fans of the genre ourselves, we wrote the book that we, as fans, would want to read. The contents are primarily about serial murders and serial murderers, but there is also material about crimes and punishment, the criminal justice system, as well as some psychosocial material.

Author's Note

SERIAL KILLERS—THOSE WHO STUDY THEM, write about them, track them down, and those dedicated to obtaining justice for the victims and their loved ones—have intrigued and fascinated many, quickly becoming among the most popular genre of books, blogs, television shows, and podcasts.

My co-author and I have dedicated much of our time to the study of the criminal mind and serial murder, historically and present day, the repercussions of serial murder, and how it has shaped what we think and feel. There wouldn't be such a huge market for true crime if it weren't in high demand.

Psychosocial development, what we consider to be "normal" and where it seems to veer off course, is fascinating. What we want to know is: what happened, and could it have been prevented? We hope to dispel the notion some are "born evil."

Using the word "evil" is viewed by many as unscientific and based on the monotheist religions. Fair enough. "Evil" is used here in the abstract sense—an act so foreign to the masses as to make it practically unimaginable.

Having many questions ourselves regarding serial killers and, more specifically, violent serial offenders with personality disorders, we've amassed an enormous amount of research material. It is apparent we are not alone in our curiosity and interest.

We recently had the privilege to serve as consultants for an upcoming episode of Reelz Channel's popular true crime series *World's Most Evil* about Doug Clark and Carol Bundy. (Hello, Liz and Imy!) Even a visit to the doctor or convenience store often results in an informal Q&A of sorts. People always have lots of questions. With this book, we hope to answer questions you've always wanted to ask.

A note about the usage of terms in this text: we try very hard to use terms and phrases accurately and respectfully, with the understanding that definitions and accepted terminology are constantly changing and evolving.

We have cross-referenced facts and cited sources. Opinions expressed by the authors were formed by facts, figures, and statistics available to the public and included in this text.

We hope you enjoy this book and thank everyone for their support.

—Co-authors Nancy A. Veysey & Kurtis-Giles Veysey

I

Questions & Answers

"*IT'S NOT REALLY ABOUT THE VICTIMS. IT'S more about the puzzle—the interesting labyrinth of human emotions and human motives.*" —forensic psychologist Katherine Ramsland, author of numerous books, including *The Human Predator*.

Who was the first person to study serial murder?

In 19th century Europe, Dr. Richard von Krafft-Ebing conducted some of the first documented research on violent sexual offenders and the crimes they committed in an effort to understand the phenomenon and its perpetrators better. Best known for his 1886 textbook, *Psychopathia Sexualis*, Dr. Krafft-Ebing described numerous case studies of sexual homicide, serial murder, and other areas of sexual proclivity.

When was forensics (as we know it today) first used in a murder investigation?

"Forensics" has become a sort of blanket term used to describe many aspects of scientific and legal investigations. The ancient Egyptians used a rudimentary form of forensic pathology. During the mummification process, they removed and observed internal organs, looking for any defect or sign of foul play.

The first recorded autopsy was performed following the legendary assassination of Julius Caesar. During that time, it was observed he had been stabbed 23 times, with the fatal wound piercing his heart. Doctors and scientists in the centuries to follow made great strides in the study of forensics.

However, it wasn't until the 19th century that forensics became more accepted as a way to solve crime, aided, perhaps, by the popularity of that great fictional detective, Sherlock Holmes.

Even still, at this time, many people still believed a photo taken of a murder victim shortly following their death had the potential of capturing the image of the killer where it was recorded on their cornea; an image of evil burned onto their eyes even as the pupil became fixed and the iris grew cloudy.

Despite skepticism, microscopic hair analysis, fingerprinting, and toxicology were terms used with higher frequency in the courtroom. Forensics played a massive role in one of the most infamous unsolved serial murder investigations in history—Jack the Ripper. It would be nearly a hundred years before DNA technology would come to use in murder investigations. Many believe DNA can crack the Ripper code. Some believe it already has.

Is a psychopath's brain different from the average person's?

Between 30%–38% of psychopaths show abnormal brainwave patterns or EEGs.

Does brain damage actually play a part in the creation of a serial killer?

Nearly 70% of serial killers received extensive head injuries as children or adolescents, which, for many researchers, suggests a link between such injuries and serial murder. Some researchers believe that the prefrontal cortex (the area involved in planning and judgment) does not function appropriately in psychopaths.

What kind of personality disorders do serial killers have?

Nearly half of the serial killers present with criteria for personality disorders (psychopathic, schizoid, and sadistic). Of the serial killers diagnosed with personality disorders, 93% have a diagnosis of psychopathy.

Are psychopaths capable of being in a healthy, loving relationship?

Recent studies suggest it might be possible for psychopaths to learn to read others' emotions and take them into consideration, thereby learning how to maintain a healthy relationship, but it isn't simple. Psychopaths feel many of the same emotions as everyone else. They experience happiness, sadness, and loneliness, for example.

It is often taken for granted that a psychopath's tendency to disregard others' feelings and needs by placing their primary focus on themselves means they are happy, but that's not necessarily the case. Happiness is dependent on social relationships, which is something psychopaths tend to find difficult. Friendships, if they exist, are usually with individuals who share their same proclivities and ideals.

This situation can prove both unhealthy and dangerous (as evidenced by the homicidal codependency of psychopathic serial killers Ottis Toole and Henry Lee Lucas). The psychopath is able to put on a so-called "mask of sanity," as Ted Bundy did with Liz Kendall, by mimicking or mirroring the emotions of others, often convincingly enough to cause their partner to believe they are indeed cared for and loved.

Can love "fix" a psychopathic personality?

The answer to this question may lie in how severe the psychopathy is. Psychopathy is typically measured on Hare's Psychopathy Checklist-Revised (PCL-R), and individuals are given a score out of 40.

Those who score over 30 are considered classic psychopaths like Ted Bundy or John Wayne Gacy. (The typical criminal who is not a psychopath scores around a 22, while noncriminal, non-psychopaths score around a two.)

The lower on the scale a psychopath is, the more likely they are to develop some sort of love for people such as family members. However, psychopaths are much less likely to develop deep bonds with others.

Interestingly, psychopaths may still want to be loved even if they are almost incapable of truly loving another. Numerous psychopaths have experienced many shorter-term relationships or even multiple marriages.

Is it true some serial killers have no conscience?

It is natural when one hears of a serial killer's depraved actions to think the perpetrator must be crazy or evil—that they have no conscience. These same acts, for most of us, are almost beyond comprehension. If we feel incapable of committing the same brutality and we consider ourselves ethical, moral, and of sound mind, then anyone capable must surely be the opposite, right? In a way, this thinking is a form of self-protecting ego fluffer.

Do serial killers experience fear?

Listening to a prosecuting attorney detail a defendant's torture and killing of his victims, it is difficult, but not impossible, to remain rather detached—a spectator of sorts. But when the crime scene and autopsy photos are displayed, when the killer ticks off each and every way he brutalized a victim as they begged for their life through split and bloodied lips, each gasp of breath spraying foamy blood and shards of teeth—it is almost impossible to remain composed.

When hearing accounts such as this, we wonder how one human being could do that to another. What emotions ran so deep and unharnessed within the killer that he believed his only recourse and salvation was to be found through the spilling of another's blood? Jealousy? Rage? —What about fear? Would that be your first guess? Fear is often a precursor to serial murder.

Criminologist Dr. Scott Bonn states in a *Psychology Today* article:

"It may seem to be counterintuitive on the surface, but many serial killers are actually insecure individuals who are compelled to kill due to a morbid fear of rejection. A neophyte serial killer who was traumatized as a child will seek to avoid painful relationships with other human beings as an adult. He will particularly seek to avoid painful relationships with those he desires or covets. Such fear of rejection may compel a fledgling serial killer to want to eliminate any objects of his affections. He may come to believe that by destroying the person he desires prior to entering into a relationship with them, he can eliminate the frightening possibility of being abandoned, humiliated or otherwise hurt by someone he loves, as he was in childhood."

When asked about murders he committed, Jeffrey Dahmer cited fear of rejection and being alone as primary factors in his decision-making. His ego would not allow him to admit it, but it is easy to deduce that this was also a reason John Wayne Gacy murdered some of his young victims. Physically, the overweight, middle-aged Gacy's odds of being found attractive by the people he found attractive—young men and good-looking teens—weren't good, and he knew it. While in custody, he bragged about tricking a victim into allowing him to place them in handcuffs with the excuse he would teach them how magicians performed escape acts.

Are serial killers and psychopaths capable of empathy?

There are more opinions on the ability of serial killers and psychopaths to empathize and data to support those opinions than there are serial killers and psychopaths. First things first—not all serial killers are psychopaths, and not all psychopaths are serial killers. The serial killers and "psychopaths" people are generally referring to oftentimes merely exhibit psychopathic or sociopathic traits.

Dennis Rader's flat affect and monotone voice during his courtroom confession were, and still are, chilling. That is the type of image in most people's minds when posing questions such as this.

One diagnostic tool, the Hare test, also known as the Psychopathy Checklist (PCL or PCL-Refined), assists with the diagnostic aspect of psychopathy and other antisocial personality disorders. The results are so remarkably accurate that the subject's test score is often factored into the decision on the length of sentence for those found guilty of violent crimes.

Developed by Dr. Robert D. Hare, a researcher and professor renowned in the field of criminal psychology, the study was initially done on prisoners already convicted of violent crimes. The test results offer proof that if most serial killers are psychopaths, the majority certainly don't test as such. Hare began his study with inmates already serving time for violent offenses.

For decades, the general consensus seemed to be serial killers lack the ability to feel much of anything at all, which is how they are able to commit violent acts with cold brutality. Recent studies, however, suggest that not only are they capable of feeling empathy, but they are also able to switch the emotion on and off at will.

This ability could explain why serial killers are charming one moment and terrifying the next, with people describing such a palpable change that they seemed to be a completely different person. It was nearly impossible to convince many of Ted Bundy's associates he was indeed the same Ted abducting and murdering young women. As a matter of fact, several of his supporters remained adamant about his innocence even after the state of Florida put him to death.

Is it possible for antisocial personality disorders such as sociopathy to be passed down to one's children?

In the context of the nature vs. nurture debate, a study was conducted that focused on a group of sociopaths who had been adopted as infants. The results showed that the biological relatives of sociopaths were 4–5 times more likely to be sociopathic than the average person. Researchers cited these results as further proof that it is easier for "bad seeds to blossom in bad environments."

What is the primary motive for serial murder?

Serial killers' motives are usually based on psychological—often sexual—gratification, though the motives may also include anger, thrill, money, and attention-seeking.

What is the MacDonald Triad?

Named for the researcher John M. Macdonald, the Macdonald Triad—also called the "evil," "homicidal," or the "Hellman and Blackman" Triad—stems from a 1963 article Macdonald published titled, *The Threat to Kill*, in which he discussed that in addition to "a history of great parental brutality" and "extreme maternal seduction," there were also three behaviors exhibited during childhood that were predictive factors in subsequent violent behavior, especially when two or more are present.

These behaviors included extreme cruelty to animals, fire setting, and bedwetting. Over time, the MacDonald Triad became accepted as a standard in the fields of forensics and psychology, even being taught in universities. The problem is, the triad has proved to be compelling but far from fault-free and accurate.

In 2009, Dr. Kori Ryan published *The Macdonald Triad: Predictor of Violence or Urban Myth*, in which she examined the triad's origins and evolution. According to her findings, there is limited clinical support for Macdonald's conclusions.

What are the stages of serial killer activity?

Dr. Joel Morris, psychologist and a founding member of the International Committee of Neuroscientists to Study Episodic Aggression, has distinguished seven different phases of serial killer activity.

Stage one is titled the "aura" stage. This stage includes daydreams and fantasies about committing the murder and carrying out the crime.

The second stage is known as the "trolling" stage. This is the time in which the killer goes out to find their potential victim, essentially hunting them down, and makes initial contact with them.

The third stage of the serial killer's activity is known as the "wooing" stage. This is the point in which, after trolling and hunting out their "prey," they lure the victim into their clutches.

The fourth stage is the actual capture of their victim.

The fifth stage is the actual act of murder itself.

The sixth stage of the killer's activity after the kill is known as the "totem" stage, which is when the killer collects trophies or souvenirs of the murder. They take something to remind them of the person or the crime itself—an article of clothing or jewelry from the victim, or something from the scene.

The seventh and final stage of the serial killer's activity is known as the "depression" stage, the post-homicidal deflation. They have finished what they set out to do and are now drained of whatever energy had compelled them to commit the murder in the first place.

Is there anything sexually unusual about the common serial killer?

Many serial killers report having an abnormally strong sex drive, and many fantasized about dead women rather than living ones. The majority related a history of intense sexual urges beginning around eight years of age and violent images already causing them to be aroused. By the time they began murdering victims, most serial killers have already acted out many of their violent fantasies with younger members of their family or with acquaintances. The link between violence and sex in those who go on to become serial rapists and serial killers is well documented.

Is it common for serial killers to have substance abuse issues?

According to the FBI, more than 70% of serial killers experienced problems related to substance abuse. While only a few serial killers were actually addicted, the majority had begun using alcohol and other substances at a very young age.

Is it common for serial killers to have problems with their mothers?

After examining ten murder cases featured in the UK series *Murderers and their Mother*, criminologist Dr. Elizabeth Yardley concluded behavior by the mothers contributed to killers' crimes, citing:

> *"The mothers of the Fred West, Robert Black, Joachim Knychala, Leszek Pekalski and Richard Kuklinksi created environments where brutality was everyday and expected. They actively abused or neglected their children, creating deviant value systems in which the abnormal became normal."*

Yardley believes that each of these serial murderers' mothers falls into one of three categories:

Anti-mothers–These women are typically victims of abuse themselves, hailing from brutal upbringings, which prevented them from ever experiencing a happy and healthy home life. While the majority of neglected and abused mothers will go on to raise normal families in the hope of taking back the control they lacked as children, some will recreate their childhood experiences as adults and become the very aggressors they had once loathed.

Uber-mothers–For uber-mothers, the issues begin outside the home, as they usually come from traditional and stable families. They are fiercely protective of their children, determined that they will not be restricted by labels that might've held them in the past, such as poverty and minority. They are the gatekeepers that hold off the outside world, protecting their child from scrutiny as their behavior becomes increasingly deviant.

Passive-mothers–Passive mothers live in fear of being judged by society. Due to their quiet and subdued nature, when their children show any moral ineptitudes or deficiencies in school and beyond, they will respond through denial, i.e., they will brush any issues under the carpet in the hope that their troubles will simply go away.

What country has the most serial killers?

The United States has the highest number of serial killers, with 76% of the world's total. Europe comes in a distant second with 17%. England has produced 28% of Europe's serial killers, Germany 27%, and France 13%.

Is it common for a serial killer to target victims of another race?

It's less typical for serial killers to prey on people from another race. With most serial killers being white, so are most of their victims (89%). That being said, let's keep in mind most victims are victims of chance. A serial killer may fantasize about what he considers his ideal victim, but most often, he acts opportunistically.

How are most serial killers apprehended?

It must be detrimental to the ego of a narcissistic serial killer such as Ted Bundy that a majority of serial killer arrests are by police officers just performing their everyday duties, completely unrelated to any ongoing serial murder investigation.

Both David Berkowitz and Larry Eyler were taken into custody thanks to parking violations, Joel Rifkin—with a dead body riding shotgun—panicked and attempted to run from officers who signaled him to pull over after noticing his truck lacked a license plate. Ted Bundy was arrested during a traffic stop for a stolen car.

At what age are most serial killers when they begin killing?

Most serial killers are young: 44% started when they were in their 20s, 26% in their teens, and 24% in their 30s.

Are most serial killers' victims chosen at random?

Yes. Even though we can find solace in the fact that statistics favor us not becoming a serial murder victim, in almost 15% of serial murder cases, the victims are chosen entirely at random.

What occupations are serial killers likely to have?

Top 3 Skilled Serial-Killer Occupations:

- Aircraft machinist/assembler, shoemaker/repair person, automobile upholsterer

Top 3 Semi-Skilled Serial Killer Occupations:

- Forestry worker/arborist, truck driver, warehouse manager

Top 3 Unskilled Serial Killer Occupations:

- General laborer, hotel porter, gas station attendant

Top 3 Professional/Government Serial Killer Occupations:

- Police/security official, military personnel, religious official

What are the most common occupations for psychopaths?

Psychopathy—or at the very least, the possession of psychopathic traits—is a common denominator among serial killers, sex offenders, and most violent criminals. Have a look at the Top 10 occupations according to an Oxford University psychologist:

CEO/business executive, lawyer, media personality, salesperson, surgeon, journalist/news anchor, police officer, religious official, chef, and military/civil servant.

How many murder victims are attributed to serial killers per year in the US?

Victims of serial killers, according to the FBI, make up a very small percentage of the estimated 15,000 people murdered annually in the US.

Of that number, only 1%, or 150 deaths, are the result of serial murder.

At what age was the youngest known convicted serial killer?

Amarjeet Sada was only eight years of age when he confessed to murdering babies who had gone missing from his small village in India. Two of his victims were relatives of his—a cousin and one of Sada's younger sisters. It was later revealed that the boy's parents knew of the murders but remained silent. The boy proudly related the details of the murders and revealed where he buried his victims when questioned by police in 2007. Under Indian law, a child cannot be tried and punished as an adult; thus, the longest sentence Sada could be given was three years in a juvenile facility. He has since served his time and is now a free man rumored to be living under an assumed name.

What age was the oldest known serial killer at the time of apprehension?

That dubious honor might belong to Canada's Bruce McArthur, who was convicted of killing eight men. McArthur is a statistical oddity among serial killers, as it is believed he began killing after the age of 60. It is rare for serial killers to remain active past the age of 55 and even more uncommon to begin their killing careers past the age of 60. A notable exception is infamous child killer Albert Fish, who was in his mid-sixties when arrested.

Has a minor ever been sentenced to death for serial murder?

Since the 1976 Supreme Court ruling that the death penalty did not violate the Eighth Amendment's prohibition against cruel and unusual punishment, 22 people have been executed for crimes committed while they were under the age of 18. All were male, and all of these, except one, were 17 years of age when the crime occurred, with all being over the age of 18 at the time of execution.

Do all serial killers have a high IQ?

According to data collected by the Serial Killer Information Center created by Dr. Mike Aamodt, the average serial killer has an IQ of 94.7. Although various tests measure IQ, a score of 90 to 110 is usually considered "average" intelligence. A serial killer with an average IQ is also the most likely to strangle or shoot their victims.

Serial killers who have used bombs show, on average, higher IQs, while those who used poison exhibited the lowest.

What is the revised definition of serial murder?

In response to criticism of previous definitions of what qualifies as serial murder, the US Department of Justice now states serial murder involves at least two different murders that occur "over a period of time ranging from hours to years."

Why would a serial killer, diagnosed as psychopathic or schizophrenic, not automatically be considered not guilty of first-degree murder by reason of diminished capacity—commonly referred to as "insanity"?

As psychologist and criminology professor Dr. Scott Bonn notes:

> *"Very few serial killers suffer from any mental illness to such a debilitating extent that they are considered to be insane by the criminal justice system. To be classified as legally insane, an individual must be unable to comprehend that an action is against the law at the exact moment the action is undertaken. In other*

words, a serial killer must be unaware that murder is legally wrong while committing the act of murder in order to be legally insane. This legal categorization of insanity is so stringent and narrow that very few serial killers are actually included in it."

Words such as "psychopathic" and "psychotic" are often mistakenly used interchangeably and/or incorrectly. A person who kills during a "psychotic" episode is acting in response to a mental state, which might (or might not) cause them to involuntarily commit a violent act.

Schizophrenics have been known to commit murder while experiencing delusional symptoms that made them fear for their life, believing they are killing in self-defense. Patients diagnosed with schizophrenia might believe they are being guided by outside forces—such as a higher power—to kill in order to protect themselves or others.

A defendant's state of mind at the time of the murder must be evaluated and unequivocally established by mental health practitioners. It is possible that a defendant, feeling there was no other recourse except murder, could then be found guilty of manslaughter or even not guilty due to diminished capacity, but it is a difficult defense to argue.

Why are serial killers primarily white?

One explanation is that white serial killers are covered more extensively in the media. Try naming five white serial killers. Pretty easy, huh? Now try naming five African American serial killers. Moreover, although we have a preconceived notion of what most serial killers "look like," statistics show that, for the most part, the racial diversity of serial killers generally mirrors that of the overall US population.

Has there ever been a case of serial killing siblings?

Although less commonly heard of, there have been several sets of serial killer siblings. The Clark brothers, Bradfield and Hadden, possessed a unique form of sibling rivalry. In July 1984, Bradfield murdered, dismembered, and consumed a dinner guest. Jealous of the attention being paid to his older brother, Hadden confessed to multiple murders, including that of a six-year-old girl.

Reggie and Ronnie Kray ran protection rackets, illegal gambling operations, and other strong-arm moneymakers, in addition to making "problems disappear" in London's swinging 60s.

The third pair of siblings convicted of serial murder, the Gonzalez sisters of Mexico, will be covered more in-depth in a later chapter.

What are the odds of being murdered by a serial killer?

FBI statistics show that less than 0.01% of murders are serial incidents. In fact, even with a homicide rate of 3.9 per 100,000, you've got only a 0.00039% chance of being a serial killer's victim. The number of serial killers is also declining.

Thanks to advancements in DNA and law enforcement, most killers are found after their second murder, never becoming a prolific serial killer with five or more killings.

Our culture has also changed, with people less likely to hitchhike or let a child ride a bicycle alone in a park. It's simply more difficult for serial killers to find vulnerable victims.

Is there a "killer" gene?

Viewers of the popular television show *Riverdale* have been asking for months now if there's any scientific data to back the storyline involving one of the main characters discovering she was born with the said killer gene. Also called the "warrior gene," Monoamine oxidase A—also known as MAOA—catalyzes the oxidative deamination of amines, such as dopamine, norepinephrine, and serotonin. This gene has also been associated with a variety of other psychiatric disorders, including antisocial behavior.

Studies among violent inmates show a correlation between low levels and a higher incidence of violent outbursts and behavior, including physical assault and murder. Scientists found those who have it secrete MAOA, which is an enzyme that can affect how the brain releases serotonin and dopamine. Serotonin is associated with feelings of happiness, while dopamine sends messages to your nerve cells. To put it simply, the "Warrior Gene" can prevent people from having appropriate "Fight or Flight" reactions.

If someone doesn't know when a situation has become unsafe, then they are more likely to remain involved in danger and potentially make poor choices. It's unlikely for women to have MAOA because it is most commonly found on the X chromosome. Because women have XX chromosomes, MAOA would not have the same effect. Barring a major plot twist, it sounds as if the

Riverdale character, Betty Cooper, does *not* carry the serial killer gene.

Is it possible to predict who will become a serial killer?

The short answer is no. At least not yet. Although science has come a long way in providing us with data showing commonalities among serial killers, the truth is, there is still much we don't know.

California's Ed Kemper has perhaps done the most in educating medical, law enforcement, and research communities by providing a first-person account of what led up to his crime spree. There have been other serial killers who provided information but not as in-depth.

There has been much hype surrounding the Macdonald Triad as a predictive tool, with studies on the long-term effects of violence and abuse during childhood and even interviews with the killers themselves offering insight, but the overwhelmingly-inconsistent results mean much is still unknown.

If a serial killer were a police officer or government agent, would they be capable of avoiding detection due to their training?

It seems logical that killer cops would know how to evade capture. That's exactly what *The Golden State Killer* did for decades.

Arrested at the age of 72, former police officer Joseph DeAngelo is suspected of murdering at least a dozen people and committing over four dozen rapes. The assaults seemingly ended abruptly, and DeAngelo remained undetected for almost three decades. It is possible he continued killing and/or assaulting women, but those crimes have simply never been linked to him. It is also possible that with the advent of DNA testing and increasing technology used to fight crime, he stopped out of fear.

Perhaps the most disturbing serial killer cop is Gennady Mikhasevich. Found guilty of murdering 36 women in the USSR, it is believed the actual number is twice that. Often assigned to investigate the very murders he committed, he pinned the murders on innocent men who were then convicted and sent to labor camps.

After a confession coerced through torture, at least one innocent man was convicted and executed. Mikhasevich became concerned once fellow officers detected a pattern to the crimes, leading them to believe they were all committed by one person rather than several individuals. Worried he would be found out, Mikhasevich sent an anonymous letter to the police stating it was the corruption of the times that resulted in the killings. But this plan backfired, and after another note was left next to a new victim, police compared the letter to the handwriting of over half a million males in the city of Oblast. The analysis pointed to Mikhasevich as the prime suspect, and he was finally taken to prison, where reports say he committed suicide.

Why do people seem shocked to learn their neighbor, co-worker, or other acquaintance is a serial killer?

Despite what you might think, people want to believe the best of others. On the flip side, people also don't like to believe they've been fooled. It could even be that, subconsciously, they realize how easily they might've been among the victims, a thought so terrifying they refuse to even acknowledge it. The brain plays many games for the sake of self-preservation and sanity.

How do serial killers decide on a victim?

No one knows for sure why a serial killer will choose a certain individual as their victim. When asked why, serial killers give a wide range of answers regarding the reasons for their murders.

The most common belief is that the killer wants to feel complete control over another person. They thrive on the fear their victims display and see murder as the ultimate form of dominance over a human.

Many agree that serial killers have a fantasy of their victims. This person would be thought of as their "ideal victim" based on race, gender, physical characteristics, or some other specific quality. It is rarely possible for the killers to find people who meet these exact qualifications, so they generally seek out people with similar traits. Therefore, serial killings often seem to be completely random at first—each victim may have something in common that only the killer easily recognizes.

How does a serial killer choose a first victim?

It is generally accepted that most serial killers feel a strong urge to commit acts of murder. They are, however, thought to be extremely cautious people who will not choose a victim unless they feel the chances of success are very high. For this reason, the first murder victim is very often a prostitute or homeless person, someone that the killer can attack without drawing a lot of attention. These factors make it even more difficult to establish patterns in a series of slayings and to track down the responsible culprit.

Where do serial killers find their victims?

Being mainly opportunistic, serial killers might choose a particular location to find a victim based on victim type but seldom have a specific, predetermined victim in mind.

A murderous pedophile might stake out a local park or playground, while a serial killer trolling prostitutes will know where to find the most desperate individuals, in the darkest and most deserted section, where no one would even think about interfering.

As criminologist Dr. James Levin states, serial killers also have a certain skill set, which aids them with the commission and concealment of their crimes.

"They have street smarts. They have a gift of staying out prison, so they can stay out on the loose for decades. Most murders are solved within 48 hours. But serial killers can stay on the loose for long

periods of time. Most serial killers are quite organized. They approach the crime scene in an organized way—carrying a weapon with them, waiting for the optimum moment to strike, so as not to be seen by eyewitnesses. When they leave the crime scene, they either clean it, or sometimes carry the victim's body to a dump site, so the body isn't found for a considerable period of time. That gives them the advantage. Serial killers also have a skill for presentation of self: impression management. They can look like the most innocent person you would ever meet. If you're a serial killer and you look so innocent, it helps you get away with murder."

Do all serial killers have a history of childhood abuse?

While it's true that the vast majority of all serial killers suffered childhood trauma, there's a problem with the theory that all children exposed to abuse will become serial killers.

If 100 kids grow up in an abusive foster home, and one turns out to be a serial killer—what about the other 99? They grew up to be, well, maybe not all well-adjusted citizens, but certainly not serial killers. The crux of the matter is finding out what caused this particular individual to kill.

Are serial killers ever found "insane" and unable to resist their compulsion to kill?

During the first big wave of "celebrity" serial killers in the 1960s and 1970s, some defense lawyers tried to argue in court that serial killers are not guilty by reason of insanity because an "irresistible compulsion to kill" is a form of temporary insanity.

The legal definition of insanity is "an inability to distinguish right from wrong and an inability to understand the consequences of an action."

Serial killers tend to be cautious and very aware of what they are doing. That's why they disguise themselves, hide evidence, and flee the scene of the crime. The acts these individuals perpetrate seem beyond our understanding and crazy to us, but the legal requirements for an insanity defense are rarely met.

Are all serial killers psychopaths?

No, that's a mistaken assumption generally played up by the media. Not all serial killers are psychopaths, and not all psychopaths are serial killers.

What treatments are used for psychopathy, and how effective are they?

An online article by award-winning writer Natasha Tracy notes:

> *"The traditional view on the treatment of psychopaths is that treatment just doesn't work. Study after study has shown that the behaviors of the psychopath do not change in response to psychoanalysis, group therapy, client-centered therapy, psychodrama, psychosurgery, electroconvulsive therapy (ECT), or drug therapy. In fact, in one very disturbing study in 1991, those psychopath inmates who were a part of group therapy actually had a higher violent recidivism rate than those psychopaths who received no therapy."*

Tracy sums things up with the rather chilling and disturbing quote from a psychopath: *"These programs are like a finishing school. They teach you how to put the squeeze on people."*

How common is it for a serial killer to turn themselves in and confess to their crimes?

We have been led to believe—again, often thanks to the media—that when a serial killer is apprehended, they intentionally left clues to their identity, that they wanted to be caught. I don't buy that. With the exception of Edmund Kemper, who not only called from a phone booth and confessed to serial murder after patiently awaiting arrest once police found the confession he left behind—no one had found the letter—he politely waited for law enforcement to arrive and take him into custody. I believe Kemper when he says he turned himself in because he knew it was the only way he would stop killing young women.

For the most part, serial killers relish the thought that they are smarter than the police and take delight in evading arrest. They don't want to stop, nor do they want to be stopped.

Is serial killing an addiction similar to smoking and drinking?

There were bowls made from human skulls, a chair reupholstered using human skin, and a very literal death mask. Although it required considerable time and patience, the seemingly mild-mannered gentleman slowly pulled the skin away from the sinew and muscle beneath before carefully crafting it into a mask he would wear as he paraded amongst the other trophies he had collected. When questioned what drove him to commit such nightmarish acts, the soft-spoken Ed Gein replied: *"I had a compulsion to do it."*

In 2015, Dr. Hanna Pickard published *Psychopathology and the Ability to Do Otherwise*, addressing the absurd notion proposed by some researchers that psychopaths—including psychopathic serial killers—have an uncontrollable urge, an irresistible compulsion the same as that of a drug addict. As Pickard points out, although an addiction seems impossible to resist, that's rarely the case. Free will still exist.

If a person—barring a medical condition rendering them unable to reason—is capable of deferring an action due to the immediate danger of being caught, then the compulsion isn't irresistible.

That being said, killers can become psychologically "addicted" to killing. Serial killers often describe the "rush" they get from murder. Some, like Manson Family member Susan Atkins, claimed the orgiastic feeling is actually "better than sex." This "rush" may be the resultant surge of adrenaline from the stressful event, followed by a rush of endorphins—the "feel good" hormone—as the killer's mind perceives the deed is done and their victim no longer a threat.

Why do people commit cannibalism?

Ressler: "Do you have any idea at all, of what would start bringing this type of fantasy to mind?"

Dahmer: "It all revolved around having complete control. Why or where it came from, I don't know."

—*How to Interview a Cannibal*, Robert K. Ressler

According to Dr. George Palermo, a forensic psychiatrist at the Medical College of Wisconsin in Milwaukee, who worked on the Jeffrey Dahmer case:

> *"It goes back to the old days of the warrior, where they would defeat their enemy and eat the part they most admired, like their brain or their heart. It's like they're saying, I really killed you. The only way you exist is in me."*

Cannibalism practices have been recorded since the middle ages, and ancient warriors are known to have consumed their conquered foe. But there are other, vast cultural reasons for consuming human flesh. While some cultures believe consuming parts of the dearly departed honors them, others believe that, by consuming the deceased, they incorporate the person's admirable qualities within themselves.

Dahmer proclaimed to believe in the act of incorporation, but his motives might have been of a more sinister bent. Dahmer voiced the belief that consuming his victims would bind their souls to him for eternity—perhaps as sexual slaves in the afterlife.

The reason for cannibalization as a means of survival is borne out by real-life stories of survival in which survivors, driven by the indomitable will to live, consumed friends and family as a last-ditch effort to stave off certain death. While the thought of eating human flesh—let alone the flesh of loved ones—pushes our limits of understanding, we nevertheless generally agree the tough decision they were forced to make did not come easy.

In three well-known incidents of cannibalism, weather and the elements were the key factors in sealing the fate of the people involved, both alive and dead. In the fourth case, well, read on to find out.

In 1846, the Donner Party set off to start new lives in California. The expedition got off to a late start, but they didn't heed the warning not to leave so late in the season. This was their first fatal mistake. They were also warned against veering off the trail, but the party proceeded with their animals and covered wagons along an uncharted trail into increasingly poor weather conditions. By this time, most of their supplies had been lost along the trail. After a month of being trapped by the cold and snow, a small group set out in the hope of getting help but returned after days of aimless and fruitless wandering. As members of the party died from starvation and exposure, the decision was made to cannibalize the dead. Of the 81 people who began the journey together, only 45 survived.

Another example of survival cannibalism concerns the 1972 plane crash made famous by the movie *Alive*. Onboard were 45 people, including a Uruguayan rugby team on their way to a match, their friends, and their family. Weather played a factor in the crash, which occurred on a particularly treacherous portion of the Andes Mountains. Camping out in what remained of the fuselage, the survivors fought a losing battle at staving off death by hypothermia, a condition compounded by starvation. The decision was made to eat the flesh of the deceased.

More than two months after being stuck in the remote snowy region, two survivors were finally able to make the ten-day trek for help. The weather was still so bad, and the men so weak, that by the time they saw a man tending his herd of livestock, they were only able to get within shouting distance. The one word the man shouted was all they needed to hear: *"Tomorrow."*

After 72 days, the group was finally rescued by helicopters, the only means of transportation able to navigate the terrain and weather conditions.

The third historical account of cannibalism as a means of survival concerns the infamous frontiersman Alfred Packer—a darling of the great state of Colorado, where, in 1967, University of Colorado students voted to name their cafeteria in his honor along with the phrase, *"Have a friend for lunch!"*

While the first two accounts leave little doubt the decision to cannibalize the dead was a brutal last-ditch effort to save their own lives—Packer's story seems less like a necessity and more like a choice. Alfred Packer was a pathological liar, and like most pathological liars, he just couldn't seem to keep his story straight. In the rough winter during the expedition, the men, ill-prepared for the trek, reportedly burned through their food rations in little time.

After wandering out of the wilds of Colorado with a cluster of his dead and eaten expedition party behind him, Packer was eventually found guilty of the murder of one of the men. Though Packer was later exonerated, the truth behind the murders of the five men still remains a mystery.

While Alfred Packer's story can be argued to be a case of survival cannibalism, the case of Tsutomu Miyazaki certainly cannot be. Miyazaki abducted and murdered four little girls in Tokyo and Saitama, Japan, in 1988 and 1989. Miyazaki, a 26-year-old outcast with a heavy interest in gore and child pornography, took body parts from his first and last victims back to his family's home, eating the final victim's hands. Miyazaki was arrested in 1989, at which point, an astonishingly enormous collection of nearly 6,000 pornographic videotapes were found in his bedroom and the remains of the little girls' body parts he hadn't consumed in his closet. He was sentenced to death and executed in 2008.

Do serial killers begin with more common crimes before advancing to murder?

That's often the case, and as noted by many researchers over the years, serial killers often start out with acts of arson. This was true of Son of Sam serial killer David Berkowitz, who is believed to have started around 2000 fires in the years just prior to the serial murders he committed. Paul Bernardo and Joseph DeAngelo were both serial rapists before becoming serial killers. Serial killers don't start out serial killers. It begins long before their first kill with progressively violent acts that culminate in the taking of human lives.

We don't often hear about female serial killers. How rare are they?

The Guardian posed this same question to author and investigative historian Dr. Peter Vronsky in 2018. Vronsky responded:

> *"Roughly one in every five to six serial killers are female. There are significant differences in their psychopathology from male killers. Research on female serial killers is difficult because they are fewer and harder to catch. Female serial killers have less tendency to leave bodies behind. They are quiet killers; they have longer killing careers. They are much better at it. There is a less sadistic tendency. They tend not to torture their victim and they are less interested in mutilation. But the motivation is similar—the need for control over their victim. It's not sex, it's control, though they may assert it through sexual acts.*

Aileen Wuornos is the classic example—a female serial killer in Florida. [...] Here was a serial killer motivated by pure rage. The types of predation in which female serial killers engage are often an extension or perversion of gender roles. For example, the expectation that women are in nurturing roles, caring roles. You have a category of female serial killers with Munchausen syndrome by proxy—mothers killing children, nurses killing patients."

How rare is it for a killer to be able to go a long time between kills?

Dennis Rader and Joseph DeAngelo both went decades without killing, but they are certainly the exception. Most serial killers continue to kill right up to their arrest.

How do serial killers think of their victims? As human beings?

Serial killers tend to regard their victims as subhuman, as existing at the level of inferior animals rather than human beings. In a sense, they go big-game hunting for the thrill. In their minds, their prey deserves the same fate as that of a lion or a tiger in the wild.

What are the most common objects to keep as trophies?

What's that old saying? One man's trash is another man's treasure? I'm not comparing murder victims to refuse—what I mean is what one finds erotic or fascinating depends on the individual.

Serial killers, like the rest of us, have turn-ons, kinks, and fantasies that might or might not be public knowledge. Lust serial killers are most likely to collect victims' body parts, but the parts they choose and why is dependent on the deviant.

Ted Bundy had a foot fetish, but in a typical narcissistic fashion, he admitted it was his own feet with which he was enamored. He did, however, like to bring the heads of his decapitated victims home and admire them—he would wash and style their hair and apply makeup in a fashion he thought suited their coloring and features.

In the case of Jerome Brudos, also a self-confessed foot fetishist, he kept a victim's severed foot in a deep freeze, taking it out occasionally to place it in a favored shoe from his vast collection.

Can serial killers choose to just quit killing permanently?

For Joseph James DeAngelo, 72, who has been charged so far with eight counts of murder, more than 30 years had passed since the last episode in the series. That long period of quiescence seems to fly in the face of the popular belief that serial rapists and killers are incapable of stopping. But forensic psychiatrists, criminal profilers, and homicide detectives who pursue cold cases say that assumption is more myth than reality.

"These are not acts that a person is compelled to do," said Dr. J. Reid Meloy, a forensic psychologist and professor of psychiatry at the University of California, San Diego. *"They are intentional and predatory. There is choice, capacity and opportunity that is exercised."*

Why do prosecutors often choose to charge an accused serial killer with a few suspected murders rather than all?

One reason is, should the defendant be found not guilty or the conviction is overturned, double jeopardy prevents the suspect from being retried. The cases with the most evidence, those felt most viable for obtaining a conviction, are tried first. Another reason, in the event a defendant is sentenced to death, the ruling is automatically appealed, so the threat of a suspected serial killer walking away scot-free is quite real.

Yet another reason is the cost per trial. The longer the trial, the more cost to taxpayers. It is estimated the trial of serial killer Randy Kraft cost the people of California somewhere between $10 and $15 million, with his defense alone costing over a quarter of a million dollars.

Why has the subject of serial murder and serial murderers become so popular?

Part of the interest stems not just from the crimes committed but also at looking into the history of the person committing the crime and determining what drove them to commit the heinous act. Through various portrayals of what leads one to engage in such violent crime, it is not surprising that there are also associated distortions and myths. We want to metaphorically dissect the killer's brain and sift through his life experiences and thought processes to discover the answer to the all-consuming: *"Why?"*

Have people always been fascinated by serial killers?

Considering the number of articles written about Jack the Ripper at the time of the Whitechapel murders and the thousands upon thousands of articles, books, movies, television shows, etc., since then, the answer is a resounding yes.

People inherently possess a desire to hear each juicy bloodlust-fueled tidbit of these lurid acts, the people who commit them, and their victims.

The advent and popularity of media outlets such as Court TV and tabloid news entities like TMZ have made millions, if not billions, off of the public's tendency to gawk and rubberneck. Accounts of serial murder seem to be the train wreck from which we can't, or simply won't, look away.

Why do serial killers become pop icons and celebrities?

In his book *Natural Born Celebrities: Serial Killers in American Culture*, author David Schmid writes:

> *"The existence of famous serial killers in contemporary American culture brings together two defining features of American modernity: stardom and violence. Not surprisingly, therefore, film is unique among popular cultural media in its potential to shed*

light on the reasons why we have celebrity serial killers because it is a medium defined by the representation of acts of violence and by the presence of stars. One of the founding figures of the medium, Thomas Edison, seems to have had a long-standing interest in violence and was also attentive to the ways in which fame could be used in conjunction with the representation of violence. One of the earliest phonograph recordings he produced featured an actor reading the confessions of H. H. Holmes..."

Perhaps the simple answer, at least in America, is that as a people, we feel we are entitled to know every little detail, and the media is more than happy to provide it—at a price, of course. We want to know what beauty regimen a celebrity uses or their secret to keeping a sleek physique. We are consumers of all things purported to be "secret." We want to be part of the inner circle with the inside information. Why should it be any different with our treatment of serial killers?

In our society, they get the Hollywood treatment as well. *(Are there other victims—subscribe to find out!)* Let's recall for a moment the Richard Ramirez mugshot bearing his snaggletooth grimace and then once in court, presto change-o; he's had a makeover complete with dazzlingly, new, white chompers, trendily coiffed hair, stylish clothing, and the last item in killer chic—dark shades. *We* create celebrities from killers. Demand for more information about serial killers' backgrounds, crimes, etc., spurs the creation of killer icons.

Do serial killers have feelings?

The majority of serial killers do not empathize with their victims and rarely, if ever, develop an emotional attachment to their victims. Their detachment and view of victims as somehow subhuman is the key that allows them to treat their victims as mere objects. With that in mind, it is also true serial killers experience the same feelings of happiness, loneliness, and sadness as the rest of us.

Are male and female serial killers represented differently in the media?

Because women are traditionally thought of as the "weaker," but also the more nurturing sex, female serial killers are particularly disturbing to many. When a woman arrested for serial murder is a member of the medical profession or a child killer such as Myra Hindley, it goes against our sensibilities and ingrained beliefs about women.

65

When male serial killers acquire nicknames from the media, the words used are violent, intimidating, masculine— "ripper," "slayer," "slasher."

In contrast, there was "Jolly" Jane Toppan, "Giggling Granny" Nannie Doss, and even Karla Homolka, the "Barbie" half of the "Ken and Barbie Killers."

The most notable exception is probably Aileen Wuornos. The media repeatedly noted she was a prostitute and a lesbian. A man-hater with no scruples or morals who killed innocent— heterosexual—men, robbing them not only of their lives, but the paltry cash they had on them, and maybe a car or two. She enjoyed killing. That was the message being sent.

In the movie *Monster*, Charlize Theron's award-winning portrayal of Wuornos was riveting, but even this story, evidenced by the title, was biased. In the film, Wuornos wants to stop hooking and obtain a decent job in order to support her girlfriend. The scenes turn a sobering and heart-wrenching scene into something comical. We are expected to laugh at someone who's trying to pull their life together. Hollywood has often glamorized killers. That was not the case this time.

What type of relationships do serial killers have with their children?

Some serial killers coerce their children into participating in their crimes. Others, like Belle Gunness, murder their children without a second thought—usually to profit from a life insurance policy.

And then there are those, such as "Green River Killer" Gary Ridgway, who seemed to have genuine affection for their children, but their sense of self-preservation and carnal desires take precedence over their offspring. Ridgway related leaving his young son alone in a vehicle one night as he led a prostitute to a wooded area nearby, where he raped and murdered her. When the child asked what happened to the woman, Ridgway didn't bat an eye as he told the boy she had decided to walk home. Another night, he had his son along and left him asleep in the truck to go have sex with a corpse he left close by. When asked what he would have done if his son had woken up and discovered what his father was up to, Ridgway denied that he'd have killed the boy, but then hedged: *"No, probably not, I don't know."* He admitted it was possible. He'd considered it.

Why do people make false confessions?

Most false confessions arise from interrogation methods. When a suspect is told the police have irrefutable proof of their guilt, many of those people in custody become convinced they were guilty and had somehow blocked out any memory of committing the murder.

How common are false confessions?

It is more common than you might think. According to the National Registry of Exonerations, 27% of people in the registry who were accused of homicide gave false confessions, and 81% of people with mental illness or intellectual disabilities did the same when they were accused of homicide.

Why do serial killers give interviews?

In 1968, Andy Warhol said, *"In the future, everyone will be world-famous for 15 minutes."* That statement has evolved over time to "everyone wants their 15 minutes of fame," and serial killers are no different in that respect. For one thing, it offers them the opportunity to speak on one of their favorite topics—themselves.

Some killers grant interviews to "give their side of the story," while others are just lonely and enjoy having a visitor and time away from their cell.

John Wayne Gacy loved any attention and the chance to brag.

Aside from the Macdonald Triad, what other commonalities have been found among known serial killers?

A study conducted by the FBI on known serial killers revealed that of those included in the research:

- Test subjects were predominantly white.

- Usually eldest sons (first or second born).

- Most had pleasant general appearances (heights and weights were within the norms, and few had distinguishing handicaps or noticeable physical abnormalities).

- Majority were of average or above-average intelligence (⅓ had superior intelligence).

- Majority began life in two-parent homes.

- One-half had mothers who were homemakers.

- The majority had fathers who worked at unskilled jobs.

- Only five of them reported living at a substandard economic level.

- Half of the offenders' families had members with criminal histories.

- Over half of the families had psychiatric problems.

- Nearly 70% of the families had histories of alcohol abuse.

- One-third of the families had histories of drug abuse.

- Almost half of the offenders' families had—or were suspected of having—sexual problems among family members.

- One-third grew up in one location; 17 experienced occasional instability; 6 reported chronic instability or frequent moving.

- Twenty-five had histories of early psychiatric difficulties.

- In 17 cases, the biological father left home before the boy reached the age of 12.

- In 21 cases, the mother was the dominant parent of the offender.

- Sixteen of the men reported cold or uncaring relationships with their mothers; 26 reported a cold or uncaring relationship with their father.

- Twenty of the men had no older brothers; 17 had no older sisters.

- Frequently, the offenders reported that discipline was unfair, hostile, inconsistent, and abusive.

- Twenty offenders had rape fantasies before they were 18 years old (seven of these men acted out these fantasies within a year of becoming aware of them).

- Physical abuse (13/31), psychological abuse (23/31), childhood sexual abuse (12/31).

- Sexual interests: 81% pornography, 79% compulsive masturbation, 72% fetishism, 71% voyeurism.

Is it actually possible for a person with multiple personalities to commit murder without knowing it?

When the condition of multiple personality disorder (MPD), now commonly referred to as dissociative identity disorder (DID), was first brought to the attention of the general population, it was by the 1957 movie *The Three Faces of Eve*. Although the movie, based on the true story of patient Chris Costner Sizemore, helped bring attention to the condition, it made little effort to educate, and in fact, served to further stigmatize those with the condition.

Six decades later, experts remain divided over this issue. A small number of MPD patients have reported they feel they are aware of all the personalities existing within them but admit that a few personalities might remain hidden and dormant without their knowledge.

There have been some studies that appear to show it is possible for identities to be aware of the existence and activities of co-existing identities, but the ability to intervene (i.e., stop a murder in progress) may be impossible.

To answer the question—even though it is unlikely and improbable, it is possible.

When serial killers choose a victim who symbolically represents the true object of their anger—someone who has physically/emotionally hurt and/ or psychologically harmed them—why isn't that first kill enough to satisfy them—why continue killing?

In the case of an adult who, for instance, symbolically kills their abuser from childhood—someone they never had the opportunity to "hurt back"—the desire cannot be satisfied because they are still unable to directly punish the abuser. The pain and anger still remain and fester within, being only partially and temporarily relieved by additional murders.

Some serial killers seem to have a "type"; why do they repeatedly kill the same "type"?

It is true that some serial killers have a certain "type" or "ideal" victim in mind, but in reality, that "ideal" can never be realized. Serial killers hunt for victims, often "settling" for victims who are available to them, knowing if they wait around for the perfect victim, they miss the chance to quench their desire to kill. So, while they have a picture of this "ideal victim," their actual victim might have only a few of these characteristics.

A perfect example of this occurred with serial killers Ted Bundy and Dennis Rader. Both Bundy and Rader enjoyed stalking their victims, and each confessed to assaulting victims at random upon finding their intended victim unavailable. In both instances, the intended victim was not home, so the killer left, viciously took out their anger and frustration on randomly selected victims, before returning to the intended victim's home and killing them.

The reason for repeatedly killing the same "type" could lie in the deep-seated hatred and unresolved anger the killer feels towards the person who originally hurt them. For these killers, no amount of bloodshed can sate or erase those negative thoughts and emotions.

For some killers, the repeated murders of the same "type" may be in response to an internal stimulus telling them the previous murder was not "good enough," and subsequent murders are endeavors to commit the "perfect" murder—one that will quiet the negative thoughts and voices.

When a serial killer acts out his fantasy, it can never be as good or as perfect or as satisfying as it was imagined.

Has a serial killer ever turned themself in and brought evidence to back up the confession?

It has been known to happen. Police in California were surprised when Wayne Adam Ford walked into the Humboldt County Sheriff's Department on Nov. 3, 1998, and confessed to killing four women. They were even more surprised when the burly trucker reached into his pocket and began wiping his face as one would with a handkerchief—but what the killer held was no handkerchief. Jaws dropped and handcuffs were slapped on as the officers realized Ford, who never missed a beat the entire time, was rubbing a woman's severed breast against his face. Ford confessed to all four murders and to dumping their body parts—minus the breast—across the state.

How long are condemned prisoners given to make their final statements?

It varies. Obviously, if there were no time constraints placed, some prisoners would talk as long as they possibly could in order to put off their execution and extend their life, if only for a few moments. Kentucky allows a prisoner two minutes for final words, while some states only allow a written statement.

What American state has the most serial killings?

With a rate of 15.65 serial killings per one million inhabitants, Alaska ranks number one in the greatest number of serial murders per capita. A total of 51 serial murders took place in Alaska between 1900 and 2014. More than half of these murders occurred between 1980 and 1990, an era stamped with the moniker "Satanic Panic." During this time, serial killer activity reached an all-time high, with Alaska leading the country in serial murder.

Many theories have been put forward to provide an explanation for this phenomenon. Some studies indicate environmental factors may play a major role. Extended winter nights for much of the year have a profound psychological impact on many people. Aside from the psychological aspect, Alaska's cycle of extended nights could provide serial killers with better hunting conditions. The size and isolation of the Alaskan wilderness may also be an appealing factor. The seclusion provides opportunities to prey on vulnerable individuals while offering many remote locations to dispose of evidence. Alaska's population, being mostly male, means there is a high number of sex workers, one of the main victim groups targeted by serial killers.

What is the shortest prison time served for murder in America?

That distinction probably goes to Laurie Ann Rogers. A victim of battered wife syndrome, the last straw for Rogers was learning her husband raped and impregnated her teenage daughter. Rogers pled guilty to manslaughter and was handed a ten-year sentence by presiding judge Paul A. Hackney. The judge then suspended all of the sentence and gave Rogers credit for time served, telling her, *"You'll be released sometime this afternoon."*

What does the M'Naghten Rule have to do with the "insanity" plea?

A verdict of "not guilty by reason of insanity" was first rendered during a trial for a political assassination. In his book, *Sinister Forces the Manson Secret: A Grimoire of American Political Witchcraft*, Peter

Levenda details the crime and how it has impacted our thoughts on the insanity defense:

> "In 1843 the accused, a Mr. Daniel M'Naghton, had attacked British Prime Minister Sir Robert Peel. M'Naghton—a Scotsman and a wood-turner—believed that the British Prime Minister was oppressing him. [...] Mr. M'Naghton believed that demonic forces were bent on his destruction and that they were personified by Sir Robert. He fired into a carriage carrying both Sir Robert and his secretary. He mistook the secretary for Sir Robert and the secretary was wounded. The secretary walked to his home after the attack, so he was not in mortal danger at that time. However, he had very poor medical care and died shortly thereafter from complications. Sir Robert managed to survive the attack. The Queen was outraged, and was looking forward to the death penalty for such an outlandish and willful attack on her ministers, but Mr. M'Naghton was sent to the mental asylum known as Bedlam after having been judged not to be in the possession of all his faculties. The verdict? Not guilty by reason of insanity. This has since become known as the M'Naghton Rule..."

What percentage of violent criminals are psychopaths?

Psychopaths make up about 1% of the general population and as much as 25% of male offenders in federal correctional settings, according to the researchers.

Are psychopaths born or bred?

Psychopaths are born, not bred, according to recent studies. Criminal psychopaths, as portrayed in Hollywood films by such characters as Hannibal Lecter, are people with anti-social personalities who lack emotional empathy. They can commit rape or murder but show no sign of remorse or guilt.

Why are people attracted to serial killers?

A controversial theory opines that serial killers, as a prototype of the alpha male, tend to attract women. This is because such males were good at protecting women and their offspring in our evolutionary history.

Are serial killers a modern phenomenon?

The Centre for Crime and Justice Studies reports that:

> *"Serial killing is considered to be a distinctly modern phenomenon by some academics, a product of relatively recent social and cultural conditions to which criminologists can provide fresh insight by accentuating the broad institutional frameworks, motivations, and opportunity structures within which serial killing occurs."*

What determines the organized from the disorganized killer?

In criminology, a disorganized offender, also sometimes called a maniac, is a classification of a serial killer. The distinction between "organized" and "disorganized" offenders was drawn by the American criminologist Roy Hazelwood. The disorganized offender is usually of low-average or below-average intelligence.

Which serial killer has the highest IQ?

"The Dating Game Killer," Rodney Alcala, reportedly has an IQ between 167 and 170. His five victims—four young women and a

12-year-old girl—were killed between 1977 and 1979. His murder spree spanned several states, including California, New York, Wyoming, and possibly Washington.

What is the most common relationship between killer and victim?

Killer and victim being unknown to one another is a predominately high statistic. The murderer being a stranger to the victim is the case in over ⅓ of murders in the United States, being by far the most common.

Murders in the United Kingdom are more likely to be between friends (male) or spouses (female), depending on the gender of the victims. In the case of male victims, being a stranger to one's killer in the UK occurs in 28% of cases.

Will the popularity of the true crime genre make it more difficult for future serial killers to go undetected?

Books, such as this one, seek not only to entertain but also to inform. As more members of society learn ways to decrease the chances of becoming a victim and ways to identify potentially dangerous individuals and situations, perhaps serial killers will become extinct.

As Sun Tzu wrote in *Art of War*:

"If you know the enemy and know yourself, you need not fear the result of a hundred battles. If you know yourself but not the enemy, for every victory gained you will also suffer a defeat. If you know neither the enemy nor yourself, you will succumb in every battle."

What is suspect-based profiling?

Offender profiling, also known as criminal profiling, is an investigative strategy used by law enforcement agencies to identify likely suspects. It has been used by investigators to link cases that may have been committed by the same perpetrator.

What is the purpose of criminal profiling?

The purpose is to identify consistencies in the personalities, backgrounds, and behaviors of offenders who commit similar crimes.

Does profiling really work?

The consensus is that profiling isn't very effective, and even profiling proponents admit criminal profiles by the professionals are only slightly more accurate than ones written by completely untrained people off the street.

In 1991, former investigator Earl James published the findings of a study he carried out on 28 U.S. serial killers, which found that 61% of the cases solved were due to eyewitness accounts rather than the direct result of police investigative work.

In the past few decades, hitchhiking has decreased. How many hitchhikers were victims of serial murder?

This is another question that is difficult to answer with absolute certainty. Of the known victims of serial murder, around 325 of these were hitching a ride at the time they were abducted and murdered.

If there are so few serial killers compared to law enforcement trained to catch them, why aren't they caught sooner?

One of the problems faced by law enforcement is that it is often difficult to know one is dealing with a serial killer when many of these killers are so upwardly mobile. Several serial killers have made great use of Interstate roadways, covering a large area consisting of not only various counties but also various states when both hunting and disposing of their victims. Once it is established that multiple homicides are the work of a serial killer, they might already be hunting in a different area.

Communication between various law enforcement agencies and police departments has also been historically substandard.

Has better science (DNA, forensics, cameras, or testing) helped police, or has it, in some counterintuitive way, helped those trying to break the law?

Now that criminals are aware of many crime-solving techniques, some have become savvier at covering up their crimes and evading capture.

Techniques used by law enforcement, such as DNA testing, are well-known. In the past, an interrogator might offer a suspect coffee, cigarettes, etc., to keep them comfortable and talking while also giving them the opportunity to collect the discarded items for testing. This had been especially successful for suspects who refused to willingly provide a DNA sample.

With the rising popularity of true crime, some killers are getting smarter. On more than one occasion, a suspect left the interrogation room after collecting and leaving with every cigarette butt and drinking cup.

In an A&E *Real Crime* article posted on March 5, 2019, Jamie Bartosch interviewed criminology and sociology professor Dr. James Levin. Levin has authored over two dozen books based on his decade's long study of serial killers' minds, motives, and M.O.

The next three questions and answers come from that interview.

Bartosch: "Why do some serial killers have near perfect total recall?

Vronsky: *"Samuel Little murdered as many as 93 women, some almost a half century ago. But all these years later, he still remembers their faces. From his Texas jail cell, the 78-year-old Little recently drew color portraits of 16 of the women he killed, including intricate details like their facial shapes, eye color and ethnicity. The drawings were so accurate, they may help police identify some of his still-unknown victims, many of whom were prostitutes or drug addicts.*

"The drawings have already been linked to two cold cases, The New York Times reported. Yet Little doesn't remember details like his victims' names, or when he committed the crimes, according to the FBI's Violent Criminal Apprehension Program (ViCAP)."

"To a serial killer, his crimes are often his greatest accomplishments in life. If you understand that, you understand why he might remember the details of his crime. He remembers the characteristics of his victims because he wants to relive his crimes. He wants to reminisce about the good times he had inflicting pain and suffering on his victims. The location is almost irrelevant. The time frame is almost meaningless. What really counts is how the victim appeared during the crime, and how he changed the victim. It also explains why [some] serial killers collect trophies or souvenirs the way baseball players collect their home run balls. They use the objects they take from the crime scene to help them relive those good times they had with their victims."

Bartosch: Do all serial killers have photographic memories?

Vronsky: *"No, I've never heard that, and I don't believe that. I've seen the whole range of serial killers and some of them are geniuses. A few have photographic memories and have very high IQs. But there are just as many who have very low IQs and would have trouble remembering their own names."*

Bartosch: Do they remember details because they regret, or are traumatized, by their actions?

Vronsky: *"No. I think they use the details to relive the crimes in their minds because they enjoyed them so much. There are a few exceptions, but serial killers have no conscience. They're sociopaths. They have empathy, but not the normal kind of empathy. They actually feel pleasure when they inflict pain. So, they don't feel the victim's pain as pain, they feel it as pleasure. The more they inflict pain and suffering, the more pleasurable their experience. It's a perverted, bizarre kind of empathy."*

What are the types of serial killers?

The four main types of serial killers based on the crime they commit are as follows: thrill seekers, mission-oriented, visionary killers, and power/control seekers.

Thrill seekers are serial killers that see outsmarting the law as some sort of amusement. They enjoy attention from the media, and they also enjoy being pursued by the police. They can be distinguished from other serial killers due to the fact that they send messages to others, and they keep detailed records of their killings. Because of this, it is logical to say that most thrill seekers can be categorized as organized, but at the same time, they do not always plan everything out in advance. For that, they are also seen as unorganized killers. Thrills seekers typically use weapons and/or rape their victims before killing them. After that, they hide the victim's corpse, and they move on to their next victim, that is, unless, of course, they are caught in the act of doing so.

Mission-oriented serial killers are killers that feel they are doing society a favor by ridding it of certain people; these can include young women, prostitutes, drug dealers, or homosexuals; people they feel that society could do without. These killers are generally not psychotic. Some see themselves as trying to change society. They always have a controlled crime scene; hence categorizing them as organized makes them much harder to track. However, since these killers always go after specific victims, this makes them much easier to track down.

Visionary serial killers are people that occasionally suffer psychotic breaks from society. They sometimes believe they are another person, or they are compelled to murder by higher entities such as God or the Devil. In fact, the two most common subcategories for visionary serial killers are demon-mandated and God-mandated. David Berkowitz is an example of such a killer. He claimed that a demon transmitted orders to him through his neighbor's dog that told him to kill. Since visionary killers tend to be more unorganized than other killers, they are very easy to track down.

Power and control serial killers enjoy their victim's terror, suffering, and screaming. These killers tend to be very organized and usually have a history of childhood abuse, which left them feeling powerless and inadequate as adults. Many of these killers also sexually abuse their victims but are not motivated by feelings of lust. To them, rape is simply another form of dominating the victim.

Are there ways to decrease the chances of being the victim of a serial killer?

Dr. Maurice Godwin says in his blog, *How Not to Be a Victim*:

> *"A serial killer can pick out a vulnerable victim a mile away. Once a predator has his hands on you half the battle has been lost. I suggest that you can reduce your chances of becoming a victim by not making exceptions to the 'common sense' rules. For example, walking two blocks home at night doesn't seem all that risky; however, remember it only takes one time to be abducted and murdered. Your mind is saying the two-block walk is no big deal but, in your gut, you have apprehensions—follow your instincts—make no exceptions to the 'common sense rule' of walking home at night. Make the effort to find alternative transportation—phone a friend or family member to come and pick you up. Many times, serial killers and sexual predators target selected victims who are at home. In some cases, the predator will enter the victim's home and wait for her to arrive. If you suspect a burglary, don't go inside the house. Go to your neighbor's house and call the police."*

He also recommends safety precautions such as not having an automatic garage door opener—due to the ease in which one can purchase a universal remote—women living alone not using their full names—only initials—on their mailboxes, turning the ringer down on your phone so a burglar can't hear it ring when no one answers it, and always letting others know where you're at.

If you are nervous in a situation, call a friend and stay on the phone with them until you feel safe. Do not open your car door to anyone when parked alone somewhere. Avoid walking across college campuses alone at night or putting yourself in any other vulnerable position. Make sure to turn on the GPS on your phone to allow your location to be observed by law enforcement should the need arise, and to carry it with you at all times.

Dr. Godwin also warns to be cautious on the internet, be careful about giving away your personal information, and watch for inconsistencies in online acquaintances' stories; online creepers target children and adults. All in all, practice safety precautions and use common sense.

Is it true that serial murder is on the decline?

Founder of the National Serial Killer Information Center, Dr. Mike Aamodt, agrees that the data collected appears to confirm this, saying:

"There's no question that there has been in a decline since the 80s in the number of identified serial killers. I'm careful to say there has been a decline in the number of serial killers we can identify— there could be thousands of serial killers that we don't know about and for some reason we're not identifying today as well as we did in the 70s, 80s and 90s. All we know for sure is there has been a decline in the number identified."

In collaboration with Florida Gulf University, Aamodt maintains a database which thus far has identified 5,000 serial killers from 1900 to the present day. Using the revised definition of serial murder, the data shows 1989 was the peak year in the United States, with 193 separate serial killers operating. The number has declined with each consecutive year.

What are the theories behind the decline in serial murder?

Of the numerous possibilities as to why serial murder seems to occur less frequently, one of the best could perhaps be due to technology. DNA testing has only been around for a few decades, but advances in technology make comparisons much easier and only require a minute sample. Another possibility is that over the last twenty years, the majority of people own cell phones. Cell phone signals can be used to establish a suspect's location at the time a murder was committed. There is also the fact that security cameras are now practically everywhere. Technological advances such as these might serve as a deterrent for would-be serial killers.

Was Jack the Ripper a sexual serial killer?

To understand the motive behind the Ripper killings, we must get inside the psyche of the killer. This man really hated women. He hated them so much that he wouldn't just kill them; he mutilated and slaughtered them in the most brutal manner before putting his handiwork on display. Because they were fallen women, he believed they died unprepared, unconfessed, and unforgiven.

In his twisted mind, he was judge, jury, and executioner. By sending them straight to hell, he not only had control over their lives but also, and this was the thrilling part, he could damn their souls to hell for all eternity. It was a type of spiritual orgasm for him. He would take possession of their souls and bind them to him forever. After all, what return address was on the infamous taunting letter allegedly sent by Jack himself? *"From Hell."*

In death, he would reign in hell, where these women would serve him in the afterlife. That would be their penance. What happened to this man to cause such hatred toward women that only slaughtering them in a frenzied baptism of blood sated him?

He most likely had negative experiences with women. Maybe some woman mocked or humiliated him, teased him or questioned his virility, and thus, his very manhood. It has been posited that, perhaps, he was impotent—either suffering from an abnormality of the genitals or syphilitic complications which rendered him impotent.

Did he blame women of the night for passing on a sexually transmitted disease? Did he seethe with hatred at the thought that these women flaunted the service of sexual release he was unable to experience? We may never know his reasoning.

There was even the possibility that he was a moral reformer of the Victorian era and hoped the murder of prostitutes would put so much fear in other sex workers that they changed professions. Anyone thinking such a thing would have to be someone far removed from life on the street, or they would realize most women then, as now, are not prostitutes because it is a lifestyle they aspire to. It is part of the grim effort to survive in the poorer segments of society. Either way, he would have his revenge against womankind by taking it out on these unfortunate women in the most brutal way possible.

Do any areas exist that have never had a serial killer?

This is an incredibly difficult question to answer. There is no way to monitor each country of the world and answer that with absolute certainty. There are many countries whose names and borders are always being renamed and redefined, making a study practically impossible.

Additional factors exist, such as the inability of law enforcement to know the exact number of people missing and presumed dead, especially those who might go undocumented because they are in an area illegally. With that being said, Antarctica might just be the only continent untouched by serial murder.

What educational background do most serial killers have?

In a study conducted by the FBI of known serial killers, even though around half never graduated high school, the reasons for dropping out of school varied, and few had to do with any learning difficulty, but instead were the result of behavioral problems.

Are there any examples of serial killers who could have been stopped by the police after their first one or two murders?

Jeffrey Dahmer was pulled over by the police late at night after they observed his car drifting across the centerline and were concerned that he might be driving while intoxicated. Little did they know at the time, Dahmer had already killed someone, and his victim's putrefying body parts were in the car. The police noticed the smell, even commenting on it. Dahmer smoothly lied, saying the trash bags were garbage he had forgotten to take to the dump.

Years later, after the man known as the "Milwaukee Cannibal" was arrested for serial murder, the lead investigator read of this incident in the defendant's file. Wondering to himself what sort of idiot would let Dahmer go without checking the contents of the bags, it was much to his chagrin he learned the reporting officer was himself.

How are healthcare workers able to get away with so many murders before they are caught?

Doctors like Harold Shipman, who it has been estimated took the life of over 600 people, are not unlike other serial killers in that they are opportunists. Accessibility and vulnerability are two things most serial killers look for when searching for victims. These victims can be found in abundance in hospitals and nursing homes.

Most serial murders within healthcare settings occur by injection, with Americans favoring injections of drugs such as insulin or epinephrine, while Europeans tend to favor injections of morphine. In either setting, these weapons of choice are easily accessible and easily disposed of without arousing suspicion. Oftentimes, especially with elderly patients, autopsies are rarely performed.

Is it true a serial killer legally changed his birth name to that of his favorite celebrity?

British serial killer Peter Dinsdale was born to a prostitute in 1960. Deformed and disabled from birth, Dinsdale lived with his maternal grandmother until the age of three, at which point he moved in with his mother and her common-law husband until the two split up.

At age 19, Dinsdale legally changed his name to Bruce Lee, in emulation of the kung fu movie star he idolized. Dinsdale, now Lee, was a typical pyromaniac. He would later confess that a tingling in his fingers let him know it was time to start a fire.

His first act of arson occurred when he was just nine and caused more than $30,000 in damages to a shopping center. His usual modus operandi was to dump paraffin through a mail slot, then light a match and throw it in.

His first fatal fire occurred in June 1973. Four years later, on January 5, 1977, he torched a nursing home. Eleven elderly patients and six rescue workers were killed. Later, Lee killed a man who had slapped him for disturbing some pigeons. The pigeons were found with their necks wrung, and the old man found burned to death in his armchair. Though the death was ruled an accident, Lee later confessed that he had snuck in when the man was asleep, dumped paraffin on him, and set him ablaze.

In 1980, a house fire claimed the lives of Edith Hastie and her three sons. A paraffin-soaked piece of paper was found inside their door.

Eventually, police were led to Bruce Lee, who confessed to a string of arson spanning 11 years. In total, 26 people died at his hand. Lee was charged with multiple counts of manslaughter and sent to a mental institution indefinitely. He would later state, *"I am devoted to fire."*

II

Facts & Figures

WHILE IN A FLORIDA JAIL FOLLOWING THE murder of his last victim, Ted Bundy asked to see a priest. No one knows what was discussed, but we do know the priest advised Bundy to stop talking to the police.

Unrepentant serial killer Donald Harvey penned the following:

> *"Lord, Grant me the serenity to accept the things I cannot change, change the things I can, and the wisdom to hide the bodies of those people I had to kill because they pissed me off."*

Just as the trapdoor of the gallows opened under Thomas Neil Cream's feet, he shouted, *"I am Jack the...!"* His final words were cut off as he was hanged.

Cream, a doctor, poisoned four prostitutes in London in 1891-1892. Despite his final apparent confession, Cream was in prison for murder in Joliet, Illinois, during the time of Jack the Ripper's murder spree.

This has not, however, kept Ripper theorists from speculating that Cream may have had a double serve his sentence for him.

While many serial killers have an average IQ, there are exceptions. Harold Shipman, for example, was a successful physician. However, he is one of the world's most prolific serial killers, with up to 250 murders being ascribed to him.

Gary Ridgway is one of the most prolific serial killers in U.S. history, convicted for the murder of at least 49 people, though he confessed to having killed more. Known as the "The Green River

Killer," he had dyslexia and a below-average IQ of 82, but his murderous run lasted almost 20 years before he was finally caught.

At one point, he was a suspect for the Green River killings due to his previous arrests. Police even took DNA samples from him and subjected him to a polygraph test, which he passed.

All his victims were women, most of whom were known sex workers. When he was finally arrested, he pled guilty to the murders and even pointed out where he dumped the bodies of his victims to avoid the death penalty. He is currently incarcerated in the Washington State Penitentiary.

Paraphilia is the experience of intense sexual arousal to atypical objects, situations, fantasies, behaviors, or individuals.

From an early age, many serial killers are intensely interested in voyeurism and fetishism, as well as other paraphilia. Many will start as peeping toms before moving on to housebreaking, rape, and murder.

Unlike some people with significant mental disorders, such as schizophrenia, psychopaths can seem normal and often charming; in a state of adaptation that psychiatrists call "the mask of sanity."

Many serial killers are fascinated by authority. They have attempted to become police officers or security guards or have served in the military.

Many have also disguised themselves as law enforcement to gain access to victims, such as Ted Bundy, the Hillside Stranglers, and John Wayne Gacy.

Henry Mudgett, better known as H. H. Holmes, is regarded as the first American male serial killer.

Ángel Maturino Reséndiz, aka "The Railroad Killer," would loot his victims' homes for money and jewelry, often sending it home to his unsuspecting wife in Mexico.

The Railroad Killer confessed to 15 murders. One murder he committed using a pickaxe. Several hours later, he killed another victim with the same pickaxe, but this time left it lodged in the victim's skull.

Three decades after being convicted of killing three people, including a teenage girl he raped and choked to death with a broomstick, Kenneth McDuff walked free from prison after bribing a member of the parole board.

Born in Denmark, Thor Nis Christiansen moved to California in the 1970s and began his career as an American serial killer. One of Christiansen's victims managed to escape after being shot and provided police with a description. They apprehended him, but not before he took at least four lives.

Carroll Edward Cole had 16 known victims. He had been in and out of prison for years, having had violent fantasies about women from an early age.

After attempting to strangle several women, Cole checked himself into a mental hospital. Though doctors noted his violent fantasies had persisted, they still decided to release him.

In 1979, he strangled his wife to death. The following year, having been found at the scene of a murder, he was taken into police custody.

At the time, police believed the woman died of natural causes, and just as they were about to release Cole, he began confessing to multiple murders.

He had problems with alcohol and admitted he remembered little about any of the murders due to having been drunk at the time.

John Robinson, hungry for sex and money, killed 11 women over a 16-year period. Many of his victims he met online, using his internet handle "Slavemaster," though some he met through conventional personal ads.

His crimes were discovered after a woman filed a complaint against him for sexual battery, and that gave the police cause to get a warrant. While searching his property, they found two large metal barrels with a female corpse in each. Three more bodies were found in barrels in a storage locker rented by Robinson.

It would later be uncovered that Robinson had cashed around $43,000 in social security and alimony checks from his victims. He had also given one victim's baby to his brother and sister-in-law, charging them $5,500 in "adoption fees."

Larry Eyler was known as the "Highway Killer." In his thirties, he began picking up young men under the guise of consensual sex. Once he got them to a secluded area, Eyler would handcuff his victims before brutally beating, then killing, them. Their bodies would be found disemboweled, pants around their ankles, discarded alongside highways.

At one scene, a tire track was found, leading police to Larry Eyler. Eyler was observed throwing eight garbage bags into a dumpster and, upon closer inspection, the bags were found to contain the remains of a fifteen-year-old boy.

Eyler was arrested, convicted, and sentenced to death. He confessed to his attorney that he had committed 21 murders and offered to give the state information on these murders if his sentence could be commuted to life. The state refused to make a deal.

In 1994, Eyler died in prison from AIDS-related complications at the age of 41. Two days later, his attorney went public with the information relating to the 21 murders. Eyler's confessions lined up with the evidence at each crime scene, and police were able to close all 21 cases.

Joel Rifkin's first victim was a prostitute he brought to his mother's house while she was away. Annoyed that all the sex worker did was shoot up and sleep, he bashed her skull in with an artillery shell, then proceeded to remove her teeth and slice away her fingerprints.

Prior to his jailhouse suicide, Israel Keyes told FBI agents the person he most identified with was serial killer Ted Bundy.

Billy Chemirmir of Dallas was allegedly able to murder at least a dozen elderly ladies by suffocating them with pillows in their sleep before anyone discovered his crimes.

After consuming a victim's thigh muscle and finding it to be tough, Jeffery Dahmer bought a meat tenderizer to use before frying the victim's bicep and eating it.

Joel Rifkin continued his studies on serial killers after being locked up. He was curious to find out what made him murder. When asked if he was a bed wetter, he chuckled before answering. After all, he was a rather prolific reader and familiar with the Macdonald Triad, which suggests children who wet the bed, show interest in fire, and harm animals are more likely to become violent offenders in adulthood.

He did not, however, seem to understand the significance of what he said next. Rifkin stated he answered no because a surgery was performed on him at the age of eight to correct his bedwetting.

Ted Bundy became friends with several anti-death penalty advocates as he sat on Death Row. In his final letter to one of them, he wrote:

"Be careful. There are a lot of crazies out there. Peace, ted"

Darren Deon Vann confessed to the murders of at least six additional women after being arrested for the murder of a nineteen-year-old prostitute. After being released from prison for aggravated rape in 2013, Vann returned to his home state of Indiana.

He strangled nineteen-year-old Afrikka Hardy and left her body in a hotel bathtub. He was caught on surveillance camera and, upon being apprehended, confessed to the six other murders. He then led police to the bodies, which he had dumped in abandoned buildings.

The jury took only 30 minutes to convict Salvatore Perrone, nicknamed the Son of Sal, for the murders of three Middle Eastern shopkeepers in Brooklyn, New York.

Perrone was a failing business owner whose wife and children had recently left him. Upon his arrest, police found a kill kit containing screwdrivers, bleach, wire cutters, three women's blouses, switchblades, latex gloves, a blood-covered eight-inch knife, and a loaded, sawed-off rifle.

His basement was full of ammunition as well as a 12-gauge shotgun.

Perrone was sentenced to 75 years to life for his crimes.

When ten women were murdered in the mid-90s in Charlotte, North Carolina, they all had one thing in common: they all knew Henry Louis Wallace.

Each woman had been friends with Wallace's girlfriend or worked with him, and each had his name in their phone book. Wallace even attended some of their funerals.

During his confession, he explained how he strangled each victim to death and disposed of their bodies in lakes or near railroad tracks. He is currently on Death Row.

In 1974, Randall Woodfield was drafted into the NFL to play for the Green Bay Packers. What the NFL didn't know was that they just drafted one of America's deadliest serial killers.

Woodfield didn't become well known as a football player. Instead, he was known as the I-5 killer after he killed over 40 people along the interstate in Oregon in the early 1980s.

He would rob, rape, and kill his victims. His preferred method: having his victim lay down and shooting them in the back of the head. He is serving a life sentence.

Without any social structure in his life, a serial killer is unable to have normal sexual relationships and is thus forced into solo sexual activities.

In some cases, they turn to obsessive masturbation, as in the case of Soviet serial killer Andrei Chikatilo, who had scars on his genitals due to aggressive masturbation.

It was noted in police reports that discarded pantyhose found at the scenes of Ted Bundy's murders appeared to have been "worn."

Murderabilia, also known as murderbilia, is a term identifying collectibles related to murders, homicides, the perpetrators, or other violent crimes.

The term was coined by Andy Kahan, director of Houston Police Department's Crime Victims Office.

KORN front man Jonathan Davis had a collection of murderabilia but decided to sell it off.

"There's definitely a vibe and weird shit attached to those things," he told World Entertainment News Network. *"I really don't want to glorify these people and what they did and display the shit. [...] When I started to think about it, I was like, 'What about those 70 girls' parents—their babies got killed in [Ted Bundy's] car, and I wanna display it! That is fucked up."*

Though it is relatively uncommon in many countries to be executed for any crime other than murder, it wasn't always that way. Many thieves, for example, were sentenced to death following their crimes.

One such case was the execution of Benjamin Beckonfield in England in 1750 for the theft of one hat.

After he slaughtered his victims, H. H. Holmes would often sell their skeletons to unwitting medical schools, which would use them for research.

John Robinson's first arrest was in 1969, at the age of 26, when it was discovered he forged documents and certificates in order to get a job as an X-ray technician at a doctor's office. While working there, he stole $33,000, for which he was arrested.

Yang Xinhai left his mark on society through a short-lived but prolific killing spree. Between 1999 and 2003, Xinhai murdered 67 and raped 23, using a hammer to bludgeon his victims to death. At times, he would kill entire families after breaking into their home in the dead of night.

He would later confess to police that he killed because he liked it, and after he'd committed a murder, he had the urge to commit another, continuing in a deadly loop until he was caught during a nightclub bust.

"I don't care whether they deserved to live or not," he said. *"It is none of my concern."*

Ahmad Suradji killed 42 women and girls and earned himself the title of "Black Magic Killer." It all started in 1986 after his dead father appeared to him in a dream and told him to kill 70 women.

Suradji was known locally as a witch doctor, which meant women came to him for help. Once they came, Suradji took them into a field and buried them up to the waist before strangling them to death. After his victims were dead, he would drink their saliva to increase his magical powers, then bury them with their heads pointing toward his house.

He was arrested in 1998 before he could see his plans through and executed a decade later by firing squad.

There was something familiar to the 911 operator about the caller's voice. Once heard, it will always be remembered. He was even given the nickname "Weepy Voice Killer."

Paul Michael Stephani had already murdered three women, calling 911 after each one and reporting his crimes in a distinctive high-pitched voice. That night, though, he was calling to report an attack on himself. His would-be victim number four smashed him in the face with a glass bottle and managed to escape.

Serial killer Richard Biegenwald was already displaying troubling behavior at the age of 5, at which time he set the family home on fire and was admitted to Rockland County Psychiatric Center for evaluation.

By age 9, he had developed both an addiction to gambling as well as alcohol. Car theft and burglary would soon follow, as did multiple murders.

Serial killer Arthur Gary Bishop attended church as a boy, even traveling as a missionary when he got older. As a young man, Bishop volunteered his time in the Big Brother mentoring program. It was here he began abusing children, eventually murdering several to ensure their silence.

Milwaukee was home to another serial killer besides Jeffrey Dahmer. Richard E. Ellis was raping and murdering women around the same time Dahmer was committing his crimes.

Donald Leroy Evans confessed to killing 70 people in parks spread across 20 states. So far, only 3 of those have been confirmed.

Professional thief Gary Charles Evans pulled several impressive capers stealing jewelry and antiques. In 1998, Evans was arrested and confessed to five murders, leading police to the scattered bodies of his dismembered victims.

His final escape was from a prison transport van. Manacled and chained, Evans used a key secreted up his nose, kicked out a van window, and jumped to his death from the Menands Bridge.

Milton Johnson was arrested for multiple murders a year and one day after his early parole on burglary and rape charges.

Prior to his murder spree, Moses Sithole had been imprisoned for the rape of a young woman, whom he later said falsified her claims against him, inspiring him to commit his gruesome crimes.

In order to kill as many women as he liked, Sithole set up a shell charity organization called Youth Against Human Abuse that he claimed was meant to wipe out child abuse. But instead of dedicating himself to that noble cause, he would take every female interviewee that he met into a remote field before beating and raping them, and then strangling them with their underwear before writing "bitch" on their dead bodies.

Michael Darnell Harvey may well be a serial killer, but he has never been officially linked to the many murders occurring in the area of Reynoldstown, Atlanta, he frequented. He was, however, arrested for the 1994 strangulation of Valerie Payton in the same neighborhood. Her nude body was found with more than 50 incision wounds that had been made post-mortem and a handwritten note reading, *I'm back, Atlanta, Mr. X.*

Police theorized Mr. X to be a possible serial killer tied to as many as seven murdered women in the Reynoldstown neighborhood. However, there was no evidence Harvey had anything to do with any of the deaths.

In 2010, he was sentenced to three consecutive life sentences for the malice murder, rape, aggravated sodomy, and aggravated assault charges in the Valerie Payton case.

"Mr. X" and his possible crimes still remain a mystery.

Carl Eugene Watts' parents must have been proud when he received a football scholarship to play his way through college. His IQ was low at 75, and he'd had to repeat eighth grade due to contracting meningitis, which set him back even further than he already was.

However, his parents would not be proud of their son's most famous achievement. He decided he enjoyed assaulting women, and between 1974 and 1982, he is believed to have killed more than 80.

Known as "The Sunday Morning Slasher," he was offered a plea deal upon his arrest, which had him convicted for burglary with intent to commit murder, but immune to murder charges. He was sentenced to 60 years in prison but was later sentenced to life when further testimony implicated him in two murders. Watts died in prison of prostate cancer in 2007.

During the 1940s and 50s, John Reginald Christie earned himself the infamous reputation as one of the UK's most prolific serial killers.

During this time, Christie, known as the "Rillington Place Strangler," killed at least eight young women, keeping trophies, which included victims' pubic hair. He kept their bodies in his home to perform necrophilia with and was only found out when he illegally sublet his flat.

The woman living upstairs asked to use his kitchen, and she happened to find three bodies behind a wallpapered alcove.

He was hung on July 15, 1953, at Pentonville Prison.

Arthur Shawcross, known as the "Genesee River Killer," was born June 6, 1945. Shawcross dropped out of school in the ninth grade and joined the army when he was nineteen.

He later claimed that, while stationed in Vietnam, he killed and cannibalized two young Vietnamese girls. After he'd arrived home, Shawcross went through four marriages, each wife leaving him due to his violent tendencies.

In 1972, Shawcross lured ten-year-old Jake Blake into the woods, where he assaulted and strangled him. Four months later, Shawcross murdered eight-year-old Karen Ann Hill.

He was arrested and confessed to both murders. He was able to obtain a plea bargain, in which he would confess to Karen's murder and receive only a sentence of manslaughter, and the charges of Jake Blake's murder would be dropped.

Shawcross was sentenced to 25 years but paroled after only 15. He quickly learned, upon his release, that his hometown was rather unwelcoming to have a child murderer living among them.

He moved to another town where, in March 1988, he took to beating, mutilating, and strangling prostitutes. At the time of his arrest, two years later, he had claimed the lives of eleven women.

He was captured when police left a victim's body lying where it was found, staking out the area. Going off the psychological profile of the perpetrator, they knew he would likely return to the site.

Shawcross was quickly spotted masturbating in his car on the bridge above where the body had been dumped. He was arrested and would confess to all eleven murders.

Bobby Joe Long was a distant cousin of Henry Lee Lucas, who murdered at least nine women between May and November 1984. Born October 14, 1953, in Kenova, West Virginia, Long's mother left his father and moved with young Long to Tampa, Florida. The two lived a transient life in Florida, often crashing with relatives or staying in rented rooms.

Long shared a bed with his mother until he was 13. His mother was overprotective and melodramatic, yet Long still managed to suffer a series of severe head injuries beginning at age five, when he was knocked unconscious in a fall from a swing and his eyelid skewered by a stick.

At 6, Long was thrown from his bicycle and crashed into a car, losing several teeth and sustaining a severe concussion. At 7, he fell from a pony and, as a result, was severely dizzy and nauseous for weeks. During his early years, Long was known for getting into fistfights with relatives and classmates.

Between 1980 and 1983, Long terrorized the Florida communities of Miami, Ocala, and Fort Lauderdale, earning the title "Classified Ad Rapist." He would prey on housewives in midday attacks, producing a knife, binding them up, then violently raping them.

Beginning in May 1984, Long strangled, stabbed, and shot at least nine victims, with a suspected tenth case he was never charged with. In early November of that year, he abducted a seventeen-year-old girl off the street and raped her but let her live. Two days later, he raped and killed one last victim before being arrested. The girl, who survived, was able to describe him and his car to the police.

He was sentenced to death for raping 50 women and killing nine.

"My only regret is that I wasn't born dead or not at all." Carl Panzram had a vengeance against the world that had wronged him. He hated everyone, himself included, and would later state that his hatred was so filling that he had no room for kindness, love, or decency.

After years of torture, sexual abuse, and beatings both in and out of prison, Panzram grew into a ferocious, callous serial killer.

He traveled the world, killing when it pleased him, committing crimes in Europe, the United States, Scotland, South America, and Africa.

In Africa, he said, he killed six men in a day and fed their bodies to crocodiles. It began in 1920, when, at age 29, he committed his first murder. He lured a couple of sailors away from a bar in New York, after which he shot them and dumped their bodies in a river.

He would later shoot a man for trying to rob him. Eventually, he went on to rape and kill two little boys, bludgeoning one to death with a rock and strangling the other with a belt.

Gerard Schaefer was a Broward County, Florida policeman with a dark secret. Though only convicted of two murders in 1973, evidence shows he was guilty of others. Clothing, jewelry, and even teeth from several missing girls and young women were found in a trunk hidden away in his mother's attic.

It is believed Schaefer may have killed upwards of thirty. He would tie the young women to trees, leaving them there while he went about his duties as a police officer. He used his badge to lure in his victims, after which he would torture, rape, mutilate, and eventually murder them.

Joseph Paul Franklin began a killing spree in 1977 at age 27. A violent white supremacist from an abusive home, Franklin murdered at least 15 men, women, and children across 11 states.

He was born James Clayton Vaughn, Jr. but later changed his name, naming himself after Benjamin Franklin and Nazi Joseph Goebbels. He was drawn into white supremacy as a teenager and dropped out of high school after an eye injury.

He got married but soon began abusing his wife. He also started getting in trouble with the law. He became heavily involved in white supremacist groups and grew more and more threatening towards minorities.

However, by the 1970s, he considered even the most extreme supremacist groups to be too tame. To bring his fellow white supremacists to action, Franklin decided he needed to set an example. He was about taking action, not just complaining, and he demonstrated by spraying an interracial couple with mace in Atlanta on Labor Day weekend in 1976.

On July 29, 1977, his attacks escalated to a fever pitch. Franklin bombed a synagogue in Tennessee, then a few days later killed two men, one African American and one Caucasian, in Wisconsin. For the next three years, Franklin crisscrossed the country, leaving a trail of bodies in his wake. He killed at least 15 people, injured six more, and robbed numerous banks along the way.

By 1980, despite his drifter lifestyle, the FBI was closing in on Franklin. In September 1980, a Kentucky police officer noticed a gun in the back of a car driven by Franklin. A records check showed an outstanding warrant, and Franklin was brought in for questioning. But he escaped while being detained.

The car was inspected, and connections were suggested to multiple racially-motivated sniper attacks across the country. The FBI sent out a description of Franklin, including the fact that he relied on blood banks for cash between bank robberies. Within weeks, a blood bank operator in Florida notified the FBI about a man matching Franklin's description being seen at the facility.

The FBI arrested Franklin in Lakeland, Florida, on October 28, 1980. Franklin was dragged through the court systems across the nation for the next two decades. Ultimately, he was convicted of multiple murders, attacks, robberies, and other crimes on both the state and federal level.

On November 13, 2013, he was executed in Missouri for the murder of a man at a synagogue in 1977.

Thirteen women, varying in age from 19 to 85, had been killed by the Boston Strangler, beginning in 1964. Each crime scene had been carefully staged to look like a burglary, yet nothing was missing from the homes. Albert DeSalvo was arrested on burglary charges, and during his talks with the police, he confessed to the murders.

DeSalvo was admitted to a psychiatric hospital in Bridgewater, Massachusetts, and diagnosed as schizophrenic. While in the hospital, he admitted to raping somewhere around 1000 women while stationed in Germany. Despite the obvious controversy of relying on admission from a mental patient in obvious duress, authorities jumped on DeSalvo's confession.

With no witnesses for the Boston Strangler case, DeSalvo was imprisoned on rape charges. He was stabbed to death in prison in 1973.

In the late 1990s and early 2000s, scientists repeatedly attempted to extract DNA from semen left at Boston Strangler crime scenes to test against DeSalvo's. However, with the difficulty in isolating a DNA profile from decades-old material, those efforts were fruitless until 2013. That year, scientists finally isolated a profile from semen left on the body of one of the victims, Mary Sullivan.

That DNA was then tested against DNA from Albert DeSalvo's nephew. It was a familial match, and though that was not enough to close the case with a degree of certainty, it did lead a judge to approve DeSalvo's exhumation in order to take a DNA sample directly from him.

After his exhumation, a DNA sample was taken from his body and compared to that left at Mary Sullivan's murder. It was a conclusive match.

In 1982, Terry Blair killed the pregnant mother of his children, Angela Monroe. Blair was 21 and had suspected his girlfriend of being a prostitute, though no evidence shows she was. Blair was arrested and sentenced to 21 years in prison.

In 2003, at the age of 42, he was paroled. Shortly after his release, he began a grisly reign of terror against prostitutes in Kansas City. After the murder of two victims, Blair decided to call 911 to report the bodies. He was unaware police had already found the corpses in the abandoned garage.

He bragged to the 911 operator, *"I put them there!"*

Eventually, DNA would be matched to Terry Blair, who had by then made numerous 911 calls reporting where his victims' bodies could be found.

Robert Maudsley was born on June 26, 1953, and was sent, along with three of his older siblings, to an orphanage as a baby. Raised by the nuns at the Nazareth House Roman Catholic orphanage until he was six, he was eventually returned home to his family in Liverpool, England.

He later stated he suffered abuse, including sexual abuse. When Maudsley was sixteen, his father beat him so severely that he finally decided to run away. Maudsley found his way to London and began using drugs, which eventually led him to prostitution as a means to support his addiction.

In 1973, he was picked up by a man named John Farrell, who took him back to his apartment in North London for sex. Farrell produced pictures of a little girl he had sexually abused, and Maudsley was so outraged, he garroted the man to death, as slowly as he could, and then smashed his skull open with a hammer.

Maudsley was arrested, convicted, and sentenced to life in prison. Upon analysis by psychiatrists, it was determined Maudsley had deep psychological problems stemming from his childhood abuse, and he was sent to Broadmoor Hospital.

In 1977, while in Broadmoor, Maudsley and a fellow patient tied up another patient, David Francis, who was suspected of being a pedophile. They barricaded themselves and Francis in the room where he was restrained and took turns torturing him for ten hours. Though hospital staff could hear everything, they were unable to get into the room to stop the men.

Maudsley was transferred to Wakefield Prison, where, on July 28, 1978, he committed his most notorious murders. His first victim that day was Salney Darwood, who was convicted of manslaughter in the death of his wife. Maudsley lured Darwood into his cell, where he garroted and stabbed him to death, then stuffed his body under his bed. Maudsley next began stalking the wing for more victims, but everyone refused to follow him to his cell. So, Maudsley cornered inmate Bill Roberts in his cell and stabbed him to death. Maudsley hacked Roberts' skull open with a makeshift knife and bashed his head into the wall before walking into the guard room, where he placed the dagger on the table and announced there would be two less names on the roll call.

When officers arrived at Roberts' body, it was alleged they found a spoon sticking out of his skull. Maudsley was now officially considered the most dangerous inmate in the United Kingdom. Prison authorities had a special cell built for him in the basement of the F Wing of Wakefield Prison. A narrow cell with windows of bulletproof glass, it bears a striking resemblance to Hannibal Lecter's cell in *Silence of the Lambs*.

Law enforcement in California had bitten off more than they could chew when they struck a deal with Patrick Kearney. He was already linked to two murders, but they had a suspicion there were more links they couldn't yet substantiate. In return for a full confession, they would not seek the death penalty.

Kearney initially confessed to eighteen murders, as well as the original two, but he didn't stop there. By the end of it, he confessed to 32 murders, and police could confirm 21 of them. Kearney had a predilection for picking up young boys and men, ranging in age from 5 to 28, and killing them. Once they were dead, he would rape their bodies, chop them up, then wrap them in garbage bags, earning himself the name "The Trash Bag Killer."

He traversed the California highways, littering the roadside with these garbage bags of body parts. Many of the remains were not found, and investigators believed Kearney might have killed as many as 43 people.

It was suspected that his lover, David Hill, played some part in the crimes, with some even suggesting Hill was the murderer and Kearney took the fall. Regardless, Kearney is currently serving a life sentence in the Mule Creek State Prison.

In 1991, three prostitutes were murdered in Dallas, Texas. It wasn't long before hairs found at one of the crime scenes matched to Charles Albright. Albright was convicted and sentenced to life in prison for the murder of one of the women.

In each case, he removed the victim's eyes, which he took as a trophy.

After his conviction, he began hanging drawings of eyeballs up in his cell.

John Allen Muhammad and Lee Boyd Malvo killed a total of 17 people and injured ten others by shooting them from a distance with rifles. At the scenes of some of the murders, tarot cards were left as a calling card. One of the cards was the "Death" card, and written on it were the words: *"Call me God."*

At another scene, they penned a 3-page note to police titled: *"For you, Mr. Police. Call Me God."* In the note, they demanded $10 million in unlimited withdrawals, and if law enforcement did not comply, they would kill off the town's children one-by-one.

The snipers were apprehended when one of them mentioned an unsolved murder in Montgomery, Alabama, in a traced phone call. Law enforcement was able to link both Muhammed and Malvo to the crimes via fingerprints.

Muhammed was put to death by lethal injection. Malvo was sentenced to life in prison.

BTK, aka Dennis Rader, spent countless hours developing his serial killer persona. He named himself the letters BTK and added a couple of dots to make them resemble a woman's breasts with legs spread open, strapped to a bondage wheel.

"The Bind Torture Kill" murderer took photos of himself dressed as a woman bound and often looking eerily lifeless. He used the resulting Polaroids, along with those taken of his victims while posed, to create a scrapbook. This scrapbook allowed him to relive the crimes without committing a new murder for over two decades.

------------◦❧◦------------

Many serial killers will keep "souvenirs" of their crimes. Ted Bundy was asked why he took Polaroids of his victims, he said:

"...when you work hard to do something, you don't want to forget it."

------------◦❧◦------------

After Ottis Toole told authorities that he often barbequed and ate his victims, Henry Lee Lucas explained he didn't take part in the cannibalistic acts. Why?

"Because I don't like barbeque sauce."

As Jake Bird was being sentenced, he declared,

> *"I'm putting the hex of Jake Bird on all of you who had anything to do with my being punished. Mark my words. You will die before I do."*

Serial killer James French's last words in the electric chair were:

> *"How's this for your headline? French Fries."*

Convicted serial killer Albert Fish looked into the eyes of his executioner and uttered his final words:

> *"I don't even know why I'm here."*

It was reported at the time "two jolts" were required to kill him, which was attributed to the large amount of metal in his body. A known sadomasochist, he enjoyed pushing needles through his skin and genitals. An x-ray from the time showed no less than 27 needles in his pubic region.

Sitting in his cell as he awaited trial in 1983, Dennis Nilsen, who murdered fifteen men, wrote:

> *"I am always surprised and truly amazed that anyone can be attracted by the macabre. The population at large is neither 'ordinary' or 'normal.' They seem to be bound together by a collective ignorance of themselves and what they are. They have, every one of them, got their deep dark thoughts with many a skeleton rattling in their secret cupboards. Their fascination with 'types' (rare types) like myself plagues them with the mystery of why and how a living person can actually do things which may be only those dark images and acts secretly within them. I believe they can identify with these 'dark images and acts' and loathe anything which reminds them of this dark side of themselves. The usual reaction is a flood of popular self-righteous condemnation but a willingness to, with friends and acquaintances, talk over and over again the appropriate bits of the case."*

Donald Henry "Pee Wee" Gaskins, an infamously sadistic murderer, was put to death in 1991. He claimed he had killed 200

female hitchhikers, abducting them and torturing them before ultimately dispatching them.

Before his execution, he wrote an autobiography called *Final Truth: The Autobiography of a Serial Killer.* In this book, he refers to his compulsion to kill as *"the bothersomeness* [sic].*"*

In the book, he states:

"The bothersomeness [sic] was getting worse. It was making me ache. All over my body. My back... all the way down into my groin. The mere sight of a woman enraged these feelings... made them pulsate and grate in the pit of my stomach."

In a letter to a journalist, Ian Bradley wrote of his partner Myra Hindley:

"Hindley has crafted a Victorian melodrama in which she portrays herself as being forced to murder serially. We both habitually carried revolvers and went for target practice on the moors. If I were mistreating her, she could have shot me dead at any time. For 30 years, she said she was acting out of love for me; now she maintains she killed because she hated me—a completely irrational hypothesis. In character, she is essentially

a chameleon, adopting whatever camouflage will suit and voicing whatever she believes the individual wishes to hear. She can kill, both in cold blood or in a rage."

After murdering his mother and her best friend, Edmund Kemper was convinced the police would discover the crimes and be hot on his trail. After a couple of days, he called the police and turned himself in. He left this note at the scene:

"Not sloppy + incomplete, gents, just a 'lack of time.'

Got things to do!!!

Appx 5:15 AM Saturday."

Edmund Kemper's older sister Susan attempted to kill her younger brother twice—the first time by trying to push him in front of a train and the second by hurling him into the deep end of a pool.

Kemper sampled portions of two victims by cutting the flesh into bite-sized pieces and using the flesh to make a macaroni casserole.

Edmund Kemper recorded over 5,000 hours of audiobooks for *The Blind Project* but has been unable to continue his work for the program since having a stroke.

Edmund Kemper was not told ahead of time he would be going to live with his grandparents. His family allowed him to believe they were only traveling there to spend Christmas together as a family. What they didn't tell Kemper was that he would be left behind. This was another thing for which he held his mother in contempt.

Edmund Kemper was known to have befriended the officers investigating the murders he had committed. Chatting with them at a bar called the "Jury Room," Edmund gleaned their knowledge of his crimes and the investigation.

When he turned himself in, the officers working the case thought it was some kind of joke. Despite being intimidating at 6'9" and 300 pounds, the man who they called "Big Ed" didn't have the personality to match the brutal Co-Ed Killer.

Following his arrest, Kemper was left alone in a room to talk to FBI investigator Robert Ressler for an interview. Once the interview was over, Ressler hit the buzzer to summon a guard. Several minutes passed, and no guard showed up.

Kemper sensed Ressler's unease and said:

"If I went apeshit in here, you'd be in a lot of trouble, wouldn't you? I could screw your head off and place it on the table to greet the guard."

Ressler managed to talk Kemper out of doing so but still remained uneasy until the guard arrived a full thirty minutes later.

Several serial killers have been known as "a co-ed killer," but Edmund Kemper is generally regarded as *The Co-ed Killer*.

When Edmund Kemper was denied parole on June 15, 1988, it came as a surprise to the prison psychiatrist whose evaluation deemed Kemper suitable for release.

During the parole hearing, Kemper calmly explained that, despite popular belief, he had not practiced cannibalism or preformed necrophilic acts on his victims but had made those confessions to police when he was tired and confused. He stated that he did, however, behead several victims due to a childhood fascination with decapitation. And, he said, he did put his mother's head on a mantle and throw darts at it as well as bury a victim's head facing his mother's window.

During the hearing, Kemper was shocked by a letter from his cousin, Patricia Kemper, begging officials not to parole him. She cited occurrences in his childhood, such as mutilating the family cat, and told officials he was still a deeply disturbed person who would kill again.

The District Attorney brought up the fact that the psychiatrist's evaluation meant little since Kemper had fooled two psychiatrists assigned to him after his release from prison following the murder of his grandparents. The psychiatrists deemed Kemper posed no danger to himself or others, yet he had already begun killing again.

Edmund Kemper was not surprised when he was denied parole this time, nor any other time he was denied.

Spain's first documented serial killer, Manuel Romasanta, was raised a girl until he was six because his parents thought he was a female.

Serial killer Luis Garavito, who is responsible for the murder of more than 135 children, will be released from prison no later than 2021 for "good behavior."

After killing a man in a restaurant, Ricky Ray Rector at first agreed to turn himself in to authorities but instead shot the police officer who had negotiated his surrender in the back, killing him. He then shot himself in the head in a suicide attempt. The attempt effectively resulted in a lobotomy. He was left so confused and disoriented, and he even saved part of his last meal for "after the execution."

In the early 2000s, the state of Florida reported it paid $150 to the executioner, $20 for the last meal, $150 for a new suit for the inmate's burial, and $525 for the undertaker's services and a coffin. In Florida, the cost of an execution is less than $1,000.

Westley Dodd, a serial child killer, once walked into a movie theater and simply carried out a young boy.

Pedro Alonso Lopez, better known as "The Monster of the Andes," was convicted of killing three young girls but confessed to the murders of 300. It was discovered he was the child of a prostitute who beat him mercilessly, finally kicking him out of the house when he was eight years old after mistakenly accusing him of trying to rape his younger sister. Eerily, his hundreds of victims resembled his sister in age and/or looks.

Bobby Joe Long believed he was receiving messages from God, instructing him to kill certain women. He also stated he only killed women who told him telepathically they were ready to be sacrificed.

In 1990, Vanity Fair published an article about a group comprised of four San Quentin prisoners: William Bonin, Doug Clark, Lawrence Bittaker, and Randy Kraft, who got together every day to play cards. Dubbed the San Quentin Bridge Club, the group disbanded after Bonin's execution.

John Joubert once said that when he was young, he fantasized about killing his babysitter and eating her.

Kenneth Bianchi, one half of the Hillside Stranglers duo, was hoping for a "not guilty by reason of insanity" ruling for his part in the slaying of 10 girls and young women.

Court-appointed mental health professionals looked on while he attempted to fake multiple personality disorder. When called out on his act, he changed his plea to "guilty" and cut a deal with the prosecution to turn state's evidence on his cousin and partner-in-crime Angelo Buono.

Lawrence Bittaker sued the California Department of Corrections for subjecting him to "cruel and unusual punishment" when he was tired of receiving cookies that were not intact at mealtime.

As with many serial killers, Richard Chase had a penchant for killing animals, though he took it a step further. Not only would he eat the animals raw, sometimes he'd mix Coca-Cola with their bodies to make the world's most disgusting protein shake.

Kenneth Bianchi became an ordained priest while incarcerated.

Convicted killer Kelsey Patterson refused to work on an appeal with defense attorney Gary Hart because Hart wasn't versed in what the Death Row prisoner termed "Hell Law."

Besides which, Patterson stated he had already received "amnesty" for his crimes by none other than Satan himself.

American serial killer Joseph Christopher, also known as the ".22-Caliber Killer," tried unsuccessfully to admit himself to the Buffalo Psychiatric Center. Weeks later, he began his killing spree.

Authorities in Sweden believed they had in custody the country's most notorious serial killer. Sture Bergwall confessed to at least 30 murders, in addition to rapes and acts of cannibalism, but the actual crime was more shocking. It was discovered all of his confessions were lies. He never actually killed a single person.

Come March 2009, investigators in Germany believed they were on the trail of a truly prolific criminal. The same female DNA had been found at 40 crime scenes dotted across Austria, France, and Germany from 1993 to 2009.

The crimes included burglaries and a total of six murders, including the murder of a Heilbronn, Germany police officer. This earned the killer her moniker of "Phantom of Heilbronn," although she was also called the "Woman Without a Face."

This theory of an unidentified prolific criminal all came crashing down later in March when it was determined the criminal didn't even exist. The DNA recovered at the crime scenes had actually come from the cotton swabs used to take samples. The DNA had been left on the cotton swabs by a woman who worked at the factory where they were made.

Serial killer Pedro Lopez killed over 300 girls and was released on $50 bail in 1998. He is currently free.

A serial killer named the "Doodler," who targeted gay men in 1970s San Francisco, would sketch his victims nude before murdering them. Though three victims survived, and a suspect was identified, none were willing to "out" themselves in open court in order to convict the suspect.

The "Redhead Murders" are a string of unsolved murders in the southeastern part of the United States. The murders spanned across West Virginia, Arkansas, Kentucky, and Tennessee, with most of the victims being found in Tennessee.

The murders most likely to be connected occurred between 1984 and 1985, though it has been theorized that bodies found between 1978 and 1992 may also be connected. All victims were redheads and were dumped along major highways, and the total victim count ranges from 6 to 11 depending on sources, due to none of the cases being officially linked.

Over the years, more than 2,500 suspects have been considered as possible suspects for the "Zodiac Killer," ranging from serial killers to politicians.

A search warrant was executed for one prime suspect, Arthur Leigh Allen, but no definitive evidence was discovered.

There have been at least three famous "Teds" on the suspect list: Ted Kaczynski, Ted Bundy, and Ted Cruz.

In 2011, New York police were investigating the death of Shannon Gilbert, whose body was discovered on Long Island, when they stumbled across a mass grave. Within the grave were the remains of four women and, nearby, six more bodies were found, including a child and a man dressed in women's clothing.

Some of the body parts, not intact, were linked with remains found miles away. Few of the victims were positively identified, but law enforcement believed most of them were sex workers who advertised their services on Craigslist. One positively-identified victim was Melissa Barthelemy, who disappeared from her Bronx home in 2009. Her family reported her missing, but police did not take the report seriously until Melissa's younger sister began receiving calls from an unknown number with a man saying, *"I killed Melissa."*

Law enforcement believes the ten victims were all killed by the same person.

The killer has not yet been identified.

Aaron Saucedo was arrested in 2017, charged with serial murder. Saucedo went on a rampage in Phoenix, Arizona, killing seven people and injuring two with a semi-automatic shotgun, between 2015 and 2016. His targets were chosen at random, seemingly anyone he spotted in the Latino neighborhood of Maryvale. His first murder was the shooting of his mother's boyfriend in 2015.

At the time of writing, his trial is still underway.

Six women have gone missing in Chillicothe, Ohio, since 2014. Many of the women were the young mothers of small children. The first woman to be reported missing was Charlotte Trego, mother of two, in May 2014. She has never been found.

A year later, 26-year-old Tiffany Sayre vanished. Her body was discovered wrapped in a sheet in a nearby county.

A task force was set up to investigate the six cases, and families believe all six are linked.

A viable suspect may be suspected serial killer Neal Falls, who was killed by an escort he attacked in 2015.

Law enforcement, meanwhile, suspect convicted torturer Ernest Moore may have knowledge of the crimes.

In the mid-1980s, in picturesque Hawaii, five women between the ages of 17 and 36 were killed. Each body was found with their hands tied behind their backs. Some were sexually assaulted. Police suspect the murders were the work of a serial killer, but the perpetrator has never been identified. The case remains open.

The Axeman of New Orleans is an unidentified serial killer who butchered six victims and injured 12 others in 1918 and 1919. A letter believed to be from the killer was published in newspapers and claimed that he would spare anyone who was playing jazz music.

Dated March 13, 1919, the anonymous killer wrote:

"I am very fond of jazz music, and I swear by all the devils in the nether regions that every person shall be spared in whose home a jazz band is in full swing at the time I have just mentioned. If everyone has a jazz band going, well, then, so much the better for you people. One thing is certain and that is that some of your people who do not jazz it out on that specific Tuesday night (if there be any) will get the axe."

The murders suddenly stopped as quickly as they had started. The crimes remain unsolved to this day.

Even with an extensive history of attempted suicide, documented mental instability, and accused patient misconduct, Charlie Cullen continued getting work as a nurse from 1988-2003 due to a national nurse shortage and was also one of the most prolific serial killers in America.

Genene Jones nearly became one of the luckiest serial killers in recent history. With 46 victims claimed during her time as a pediatric nurse, she almost walked free after 33 years behind bars.

The crime she was convicted for was the murder of a 15-month-old girl in Kerrville, Texas. In an interview with ABC News in 2013, the little girl's mother, Petti McClellan, gave the story of the grotesque crime.

McClellan had brought her 3-year-old son to a new clinic for a flu treatment and brought her infant daughter, Chelsea, along. Genene Jones, a nurse at the clinic, told McClellan she would update the baby's shots. McClellan watched on as Jones cradled little Chelsea in her arms, giving her two doses of succinylcholine from a syringe. Chelsea immediately stopped breathing and was rushed by ambulance to a hospital in San Antonio. Jones got in the ambulance with Chelsea, and McClellan followed behind. Jones gave Chelsea a final, fatal dose despite the protests of the EMTs in the ambulance. Chelsea was dead before they arrived at the hospital.

During the investigation, authorities came to believe Jones had murdered 46 babies during her career. She was sentenced to 99 years in prison for Chelsea's murder, but a 1977 Texas law would have allowed her to walk free.

The law, in a move to reduce prison overcrowding, allowed inmates to be released after serving one-third of their sentence, provided they had good behavior. Jones was sentenced in 1985, but in accordance with the law, she was scheduled for parole in 2018, meaning she could have been a free woman.

However, in 2017, she was indicted for the murder of 11-month-old Joshua Sawyer. After pleading guilty in a deal to get four other charges dropped, she was sentenced to life in prison.

The 1977 law was amended to only being applicable to nonviolent offenders in 1987, but it very easily could have let a horrifying serial child killer walk free.

Vickie Dawn Jackson, a nurse at a North Texas hospital, may have killed 20 people in the short period between December 2000 and February 2001, and attempted to kill five more. Despite her short yet high-volume killing spree, her name is little known outside of her small town.

The hospital where she worked had a rash of respiratory-related deaths, but since all the deceased were elderly, it wasn't viewed as suspicious. That is, until administrators noticed that several vials of mivacurium chloride were missing.

Mivacurium chloride temporarily knocks out a patient's respiratory drive, rendering them unable to breathe. Investigators eventually honed in on Vickie Jackson, who had been the last one in the rooms of the deceased. She had told coworkers she would "take care" of unruly patients.

Two months after her killing spree had begun, a syringe with traces of mivacurium chloride was found in her garbage. However, it took over a year, until July 2002, for Jackson to be arrested.

In 2006, she pled no contest to the charges that she had killed ten patients and was sentenced to life in prison.

Dr. William Palmer murdered at least a dozen victims, fathered around 15 illegitimate children by various women, and served as an illegal abortionist to other women—many of whom he had impregnated himself.

But perhaps even more atrocious was the act he committed out of curiosity. He intentionally poisoned an innocent man and stayed with him until the moment of death, taking notes on the poison's effects and how long it took the victim to die. This was to determine if poison was the most effective murder weapon for the evil deeds he had planned.

Gwendolyn Graham and Catherine May Wood terrorized the Alpine Manor Nursing Home where they worked in 1987. Wood and Graham, two nurses' aides in Walker, Michigan, began a whirlwind sexual relationship with themes of sadomasochism, but eventually, that wasn't enough to satisfy them. The two ultimately decided that killing their elderly patients was an alluring form of foreplay and decided on their first victim.

In January 1987, Graham snuck into the bedroom of an elderly patient suffering from Alzheimer's. While Wood acted as a lookout, Graham smothered the woman with a washcloth. By the end of that year, the couple had claimed the lives of five patients, all of whom had Alzheimer's and unable to fight back.

The two chose their victims according to their first initials, hoping to ultimately spell out "MURDER."

When Graham left Wood for another woman, an embittered Wood sought revenge by confessing to the police about the murders. The two were arrested in December 1988.

Graham was given five life sentences. Wood received 20 years for one count of second-degree murder and one count of conspiracy to commit second-degree murder.

Nurse Beverley Allitt killed four children and tried to kill many more while working in a hospital in 1991. She would give the children large doses of insulin over the course of 59 days, with no motive.

Allitt was sentenced to a minimum of 30 years in prison, one of the longest sentences given to a woman in Britain.

Anísio Ferreira de Sousa, a Brazilian doctor, killed at least 19 boys in 1989–1992.

De Sousa was part of a satanic ring that sexually abused, mutilated, and killed young children.

He was convicted of 3 murders and sentenced to 77 years in prison.

Abraão José Bueno was working as a nurse in Brazil in 2005 when officials discovered that he was giving babies and children overdoses of sedatives. Many of his victims were suffering from leukemia or AIDS.

Bueno attempted to resuscitate each child after giving the overdose, but four of the children died.

He was sentenced to 110 years in prison.

Donald Harvey was a former orderly in hospitals in Ohio and Kentucky during the 1970s and 1980s. During this time, he killed an estimated 37 patients.

The real victim count is believed to be much higher, as Harvey claimed the figure is closer to 70.

His killing spree "began by accident" after hooking up a patient to an empty oxygen tank, and then he just couldn't stop. The cold-blooded killer never showed any remorse for his crimes.

In one interview, he said:

"Some of those (patients) might have lasted a few more hours or a few more days, but they were all going to die. I know you think I played God, and I did."

Serial killer Javed Iqbal was sentenced to death by being strangled in front of his victims' families and would then be dismembered and burned in a vat of acid, in the same way that he killed over 100 16-year-old boys.

Either by providence or his own hand, he escaped execution when he was found dead in his cell before the execution could be carried out.

Eugene Butler was declared mentally insane in 1906 and died in an asylum a few years later. Two years after his death, his small town in North Dakota learned Butler might have been a serial killer.

During an excavation of his former home, the bodies of six teenage boys were found buried under the floorboards. They were between the ages of 15 and 18. They were killed by a blow to the back of the head. The motive for the murders was never discovered.

Serial killer Joseph Briggen always had prize-winning hogs at the California state fair. He'd state, *"it's all in the feeding"* when asked the secret for his success.

He was arrested when it was learned he was feeding his ranch workers to the hogs.

Israel Keyes was a serial killer who would travel via plane from Alaska to the continental U.S. to bury murder kits. He would return years later to retrieve them and kill at random. He had no victim profile.

In 1865, the *Ottawa Citizen* reported that a woman, surname Perkins, confessed on her death bed to having murdered six people.

It was said the crimes were *"nearer to the Burke and Hare murders than anything we have heard of."*

The woman, who it was reported had a *"mania to destroy human life,"* poisoned all six individuals, all of whom she knew closely.

"…She practiced until six of her victims slept their last sleep," the paper reported, *"two of them being adults and four of them children, and what makes the matter more revolting and horrid is that one of the former was her own husband, two of the latter were her own children."*

Perkins had killed her children in England, and her husband in Canada, later remarrying.

"This wretch […] lived for years past in great horror with the image of her victims continually appearing before her eyes," the article concluded, *"her cries and imprecations were fearful, and her actions, language and appearance were loathsome till death stopped her groans and curses."*

One notorious historical serial killer was the 15th-century nobleman Gilles de Rais who fought alongside Joan of Arc during the Hundred Years War.

After she was executed, he had his servants lure young boys to his castle where he would torture, sexually assault, and kill them.

16th-century serial killer Christman Genipperteinga murdered 964 individuals. This included 6 of his newborn babies, birthed from a sex slave he held captive for seven years before she convinced him to let her go into town, where she betrayed him by dropping peas for the town's men to follow and capture him.

In 1924, in Peck County, Pennsylvania, a dog named Pep was tried and convicted of killing a cat. Pep was sentenced to spend the rest of his life, which amounted to just six years, in prison. He was given a prison number (#C2559) and was very content in prison, spoiled and adored by his fellow inmates.

King Henry VIII had Thomas Beckett, what there was left of him, hauled before him and charged with treason—three hundred years after Beckett's death.

Jeffrey Dahmer described the taste of the human heart as *"spongy."*

Serial killer Albert Fish cruelly and sadistically wrote the mother of his twelve-year-old victim:

> *"I choked her to death, then cut her in small pieces so I could take my meat to my rooms. Cook and eat it. How sweet and tender her little ass was roasted in the oven. It took me nine days to eat her entire body."*

Washington state contractor Casey Clopton was hired to renovate a house in Tacoma, Washington, where Ted Bundy had lived as a child.

Clopton said the first time he came by the house with his 11-year-old daughter, the girl started crying and said the residence made her feel weird. During the renovation, workers found the words *"help me"* written on a basement window and the word *"leave"* written in dust on a bedroom floor.

One time, the crew unlocked the house to find every door inside ajar; another time, a heavy cabinet toppled over.

Clopton eventually invited two priests to bless the house; they recommended that the workers write scripture verses on the walls and play Christian music.

In the final days before his scheduled execution, after already being granted two stays of execution, Ted Bundy convinced a legal aid to speak with his East Coast victims' families.

If they would write to Florida Governor Robert Martinez and request a third stay, he would give up more victims and the details of their deaths and locations of burial sites.

Governor Martinez responded: *"For him to be negotiating for his life over the bodies of others is despicable."*

One of Ted Bundy's defense lawyers, John Henry Brown, chronicles in his biography, *Defending the Devil*, that Bundy revealed to him his first murder was as a teenager when he accidentally killed someone when things went afoul during what the killer termed *"sex play."*

Ted Bundy, having declined to order anything special for his last meal, was provided the prison's standard, condemned man's steak and eggs. The meal was eaten by a guard after Bundy declined this as well.

Before the term "murderabilia" was commonplace, Arthur Nash amassed a collection which at the time included Ted Bundy's death wagon and John Wayne Gacy's original artwork reported to be worth millions of dollars.

Fifteen years after her disappearance, during his last-minute confessions, Ted Bundy admitted to abducting and killing 17-year-old Debra Kent from Bountiful, Utah, in 1974.

Bundy confessed to taking the victim back to the apartment he was renting.

"I did keep her there for a period of time," Bundy said, estimating that it had been about 24 hours.

After the officer on the tape is heard asking Bundy whether Kent was alive during her time in captivity, Bundy chillingly responded:

"Let's see, during half of it."

Bundy biographers Stephen Michaud and Hugh Aynesworth revealed in their collaboration, *The Only Living Witness*, that they had purchased the wedding bands and groom's attire for the Bundy-Boone courthouse nuptials.

It was reported in the *Deseret News* shortly after his execution that Ted Bundy's executioner may have been a woman. The executioner was chosen from a list compiled thirteen years before, after the state had advertised for executioners in 1976. The identity of those on the list of executioners was kept hush, with only the superintendent of the Florida State Prison, Thomas Burton, being privy to the information.

A spokesman for then-Governor Bob Martinez, Jon Peck, told the press that he didn't know who exactly executed Bundy, but that many witnesses speculated that it might have been a woman.

Old Sparky, Florida state's infamous electric chair, the last seat taken by Ted Bundy and many murderers before him, was made in 1924 by prisoners from an old oak tree growing on prison grounds.

The last abode Bundy had as a free man was named *"The Oak,"* in honor of the ancient oak tree growing on the property.

During Ted Bundy's nine years on death row, he received three stays of execution. By the time he was put to death in the electric chair, Bundy had cost taxpayers more than 5 million dollars.

It is well-known by anyone who has studied the Bundy case that Bundy reportedly never got over his first love. It has even been theorized that Bundy's victims all resembled her.

When Diane Edwards and Ted Bundy split the final time, Edwards married someone else while Bundy began abducting and killing young women that looked similar to Edwards.

After Bundy's arrest, Edwards contributed to Dr. Al Carlisle's study of Bundy, describing him as a *"people-pleaser"* who *"wouldn't stand up for himself."*

"This was my main criticism of him after the year and a half of our relationship," Edwards told Carlisle. *"He wasn't strong. He wasn't real masculine. If I got mad at him because he did something, he sort of felt apologetic about it. He wouldn't stand up for himself."*

Since the interview in 1976, Edwards has tried to remain out of the public eye, concealing her identity from the public.

Ted Bundy was a reasonable man, except when he felt himself slipping under influences of what he referred to as the *"entity,"* which consumed him and prevented him from *"being himself."*

At such times, he said, he was *"despicable and inhuman."*

When Bundy was sentenced to death, he said something very strange to the court:

"I cannot accept the sentence," he said, *"because it is not a sentence to me… it is a sentence to someone else who is not standing here today."*

He did not mean to imply that they had got the wrong man, but that the murderer (or *"entity"*) was not in him at that moment, that the disruption he caused to Bundy's personality was episodic.

While employed by the state of Washington, Ted Bundy wrote a pamphlet for women about rape prevention.

There currently are 740 offenders on California's death row, making it the largest death row in the nation. Since California reinstated capital punishment in 1978, 79 condemned inmates have died from natural causes and 25 have committed suicide.

Just 13 have since been executed in California, one was executed in Missouri, and one was executed in Virginia.

A German serial killer, Egidius Schiffer, accidentally killed himself with a fatal electrical shock after tying a cable from a lamp around his penis and nipples in a strange masturbatory act.

Schiffer, known as the "Aachen Strangler," was found still tied up when guards opened his room in the morning.

Spokeswoman for the Bochum Prison, Candida Tunkel, said:

"He removed a cable from his bedside table lamp. Then he wound it around his nipples and his penis and stuck the end in a power socket."

Schiffer, 62, suffered heart failure due to the electric current running through his chest. Schiffer had been sentenced to life in prison in 2008 after DNA linked him to a string of murders between 1983 and 1990. He killed five women, one only fifteen, after picking them up hitchhiking.

He was arrested in 2007 while stealing scrap metal and voluntarily gave a DNA sample, which linked him to the murders.

Schiffer confessed his involvement before ultimately recanting, claiming he was sadomasochistic and the thought of being imprisoned turned him on.

Around 5% of serial killers commit suicide. Most often, they kill themselves to avoid arrest or prison, or to terminate a prison sentence. Just over half killed themselves after arrest.

Those killing for criminal enterprise rather than other reasons—lust, power, anger, thrill, etc.—were three times more likely to commit suicide.

Only five percent of the suicides killed themselves before they were even identified.

About one-fourth waited until after their conviction.

On March 5, 1970, the parents of three girls who lived near Los Angeles realized the girls were missing. Two returned home to report being kidnapped, but the third child remained missing.

Soon after, Mack Ray Edwards entered the LAPD station. He admitted to the kidnapping, revealed his accomplice, and gave police directions to where the still-missing girl could be found.

He then confessed to killing other children.

Before his trial, he attempted to kill himself twice. He also told the jury he wanted to be executed. He got his wish, but the appeals process was too slow, and he hung himself with an electrical cord.

Herb Baumeister committed suicide after being uncovered as a serial sex killer. He had a penchant for bringing young men home while his wife and children were away, sexually assaulting and then murdering them. He would then scatter their remains around his vast property. It worked out well for him until his children discovered a human skull outside their home.

Baumeister quickly surmised death was easier than facing charges and fled to Canada, where he killed himself while police investigated his home.

David Maust confessed to killing two boys after being convicted of the death of three others. Maust expressed remorse for the killings and, in an interview, stated that the boys were good kids who did not deserve to die.

"They had nothing I wanted except for them to be my friend, and they took nothing from me," he said. *"But I still killed them for no reason."*

He committed suicide by hanging himself in his cell in 2006. He left a lengthy suicide note, detailing his decision to kill himself even before his arrest and confessed to two additional murders he had not been charged with.

In his suicide note, David Maust stated:

> *"Before I left to come to Indiana, I made a deal with myself that I would come back and take responsibility for every evil act I committed in life (including the three murders in Indiana) and then right before the trial or right after I testified in court—I would do the right thing and kill myself because I wanted my trial to be for the families and I didn't want them to wait long for the justice they desired. For if their sons are not alive than I feel I should not be allowed to live either, and I have always felt that way…"*

Historians note that legends such as werewolves and vampires were inspired by medieval serial killers.

Boone Helm was a career criminal and serial killer who crisscrossed the United States, leaving a trail of bodies in his wake.

He was executed by vigilantes on January 14, 1864, alongside his fellow highway robbers.

Helm's last words were: *"Let 'er rip!"* Then he jumped from his makeshift gallows platform.

For his last meal prior to execution, Kenneth McDuff, the Broomstick Killer, requested steak. He was served hamburger meat.

On the night of July 14, 1966, Richard Speck murdered eight student nurses in a very meticulous and methodical manner. Twenty minutes after taking his first victim into another room and murdering her, he came back for a second victim, again, returning in twenty minutes. This pattern continued until all the young women were dead, except for one fortunate enough to stay hidden from the killer during the massacre.

Foniasophobia is the fear of murderers or serial killers, or of being murdered. This fear is usually triggered after hearing news that somebody got murdered or of hearing a person on a killing spree, or more rarely encountering people who killed other people. People suffering from foniasophobia would usually lead to anthrophobia, fear of people, as anybody could kill them, and thanatophobia, fear of death, as the act of killing results in death. As a result, s/he would hide alone in remote places, away from populated areas.

In 2014, Donald Trump was pranked on Twitter. Asked to retweet a photo of the Twitter user's parents in their memory, Trump complied. The photo was immediately recognizable to most Twitter users—excluding Trump—as being the infamous serial killing couple, Fred and Rosemary West.

According to Ottis Toole, his Satanist grandmother took him on grave robbing expeditions and made him participate in rituals that included self-mutilation. Toole went on to kill at least six people.

David Berkowitz claims the Son of Sam murders were carried out by a network of occultists working in tandem. Evidence appears to back up his assertion.

Ned Kelly was one of Australia's most famous criminals. Kelly shot and injured a policeman trying to arrest his brother, after which the two brothers fled into the bush. Two men would soon join them, and they formed what would be known as the Kelly gang.

These bushranger outlaws would commit numerous robberies between 1878 and 1880. Eventually, after many police shootings and robberies, the outlaws took control of Glenrowan township.

During the ensuing struggle, Ned Kelly was injured and captured, and his fellow outlaws were killed. Kelly was later hanged for his crimes.

The story of Ned Kelly has captured public attention since the time of the crimes and inspired numerous movies since.

In 1933, a man attempted to rob a Paris antique store while in disguise. However, his disguise was a full suit of 15th-century armor. Quite obviously, the disguise was his downfall as it woke everyone.

In the 1920s, the American Friendship Society was one of many matchmaking services throughout the United States. Members paid an annual fee and would then receive a list of eligible lovers in their area.

Harry F. Powers bought a subscription and listed an alias. The women who met with him for a date disappeared.

Although police at the time thought he was guilty of upwards of fifty murders, Powers was convicted of killing five—three of whom were children of one of his victims.

He was sentenced to death and hung in 1932.

Pedro Rodrigues Filho isn't exactly Dexter, but he was a serial killer who killed other criminals, which would make him one of the "nicer" serial killers.

Nike's famous slogan *"Just Do It,"* created by Dan Wieden in 1988, was actually inspired by the final words of an executed murderer.

Gary Gilmore killed two people in Utah in 1976 and was sentenced to death in October of that year. His execution occurred on January 17, 1977, and facing a five-man firing squad, he was asked if he had any last words. Calmly, Gilmore said, *"Let's do it."*

"I like the 'do it' part of it," Wieden told filmmaker Doug Pray in the documentary *Art & Copy.* *"None of us really paid much attention. We thought, 'Yeah. That'd work.'"*

In the 1960s, Ted Kaczynski made an appointment to speak with a psychiatrist regarding a sex change operation. He kept the appointment but was too embarrassed to discuss the topic.

Although Charles Manson was not *legally* permitted to profit from his crimes or use of his image for merchandise, he still managed to die with a net worth of at least $400,000. According to Manson's son, Valentine, the infamous criminal mastermind supposedly earned the fortune by selling paintings, t-shirts, photos, interviews, and more through various websites that he and his associates operated. However, Manson could not directly access the money or benefit from it and officially lived on a 35-dollar monthly stipend.

Suspected in far more murders than those he was convicted of, investigators considered Ted Bundy a suspect in several unsolved murders, perhaps most notably, some of the Zodiac murders.

Harvey Glatman posed as a photographer to lure his victims in the 1950s.

Rodney Alcala would go on to do the same.

The only two women in England serving life sentences clashed immediately upon meeting. As soon as serial killer Joanna Dennehy arrived in the prison where Rosemary West was also serving her sentence, she threatened to kill West.

West was immediately placed in solitary confinement before being transferred to a different prison the next day amid concerns for her safety.

It was the real-life Pa from the television series *The Little House on the Prairie*, his daughter alleges, who killed a notorious family of serial killers known as the "Bloody Benders."

Wyatt Earp may have descended from some of America's first serial killers, the Harpe Brothers, who murdered up to 40 people and even bashed an infant against a tree for crying.

When caught and executed, one brother was beheaded, and his head was left on a spike as a warning. That area is still known in Kentucky as "Harpe's Head."

One half of the serial killing pair known as the "Hillside Stranglers," Kenneth Bianchi, was murdering women while also applying to join the ranks of the LAPD, and on several occasions, was allowed to ride along with police officers who were searching for the Hillside Strangler.

At least twenty known serial killers were at one time members of the United States military.

Dean "Candy Man" Corll was granted an honorable discharge from the U.S. Army in order to take over his family's candy-making business.

Tied to more than two dozen murders, he was known to give candy away to youngsters, especially teen boys.

Ted Bundy attempted to abduct a girl while on the run in Florida. She said he looked dirty and was acting strangely. He was also wearing a plastic badge with the same name on it as that of well-known British actor Richard Burton.

In the 1980s, Christine Falling became known as the "Babysitter from Hell" after she choked and killed five children under her care, including an 8-month-old baby. She was just 19 years old when she murdered the children.

After one of his victims disappeared, serial killer/cannibal Nathaniel Bar-Jonah started holding cookouts where he served burgers and chili to his guests. He said he had gone deer hunting, but he did not own a rifle, have a hunting license, nor had he been deer hunting at any time.

In Bar-Jonah's apartment, detectives found a number of recipes using children's body parts with contemptuous titles such as *"little boy pot pie," "French fried kid,"* and phrases such as, *"lunch is served on the patio with roasted child."*

Charles Schmid, the "Pied Piper of Tucson," was sentenced to death for the murder of three young girls. After his sentencing, he tried and failed to escape prison a few times. Finally, on November 11,

1965, he successfully escaped prison with fellow triple murderer, Raymond Hudgens.

The men took four people hostage on a ranch in Arizona before ultimately being apprehended and returned to prison.

On March 10, 1975, Schmid was stabbed 47 times by two prisoners during a brawl and died on March 30 from complications.

His body was reportedly stolen from the prison morgue and never found, raising questions of whether he had ever actually died.

Dean Corll was meticulous in choosing the boys whom he would murder; he preyed on runaways and children from low-income homes in order to keep from raising suspicion. And just to make sure no one came looking for the boys, he would often have them write letters to their family saying they had left town seeking employment before he strangled them to death.

Marybeth Tinning killed her nine children from 1972 to 1985. Even though each of her children died under different suspicious circumstances over the course of a decade, she wasn't caught until her adopted child was found dead.

She was only convicted of the death of one child, for which she received 20 years in prison.

Norman Afzal Simons was better known as the "Station Strangler" for his history of luring his victims from train stations. Then, he would rape and strangle his child victims.

He killed at least 22 children between 1986 and 1994.

He was sentenced to life in prison in South Africa.

Over a period of 7 years, Ramadan Abdel Rehim Mansour raped and murdered at least 32 children. His victims were mostly young boys between the ages of 10 and 14.

He had six accomplices, all of whom were caught in 2006 and sentenced to death.

When he was just 16, Cayetano Santos Godino was responsible for the death of 4 children and the attempted murder of 7 more in 1912. He even burned down seven buildings.

He was caught and imprisoned later that year.

After killing 2 of the prison pet cats, he died under suspicious circumstances.

As the main culprit behind the Wineville Chicken Coop Murders, Gordon Stewart Northcott abducted and murdered at least three boys in California.

He was caught in 1928 and hung two years later.

It was only after his arrest on multiple murder charges that Jeffrey Dahmer discovered his father wondered if he had passed on a genetic predisposition for violence.

In the autobiographical book, *A Father's Story*, Lionel Dahmer wrote of having some of the same *"compulsions"* as his son.

Jeffrey knew nothing about this until reading the copy of the book his father sent him in prison.

Many have speculated damage might have occurred in vitro due to the medication his mother was on at the time. Dahmer did not subscribe to either theory.

He stated that blaming one's parents for the situations you create is nothing more than a *"cop out."*

While stationed in the Army in Germany, it appears Jeffery Dahmer's sadistic tendencies did not cease. After his arrest, German law enforcement visited him to question him about the unusual slate of murders in the radius of the base he was stationed at. Naturally, they could not tie him to the murders very easily, as all the victims were women, and his typical victim profile was young men.

Dahmer was caught twice by military police during his time in Germany masturbating publicly in front of children. He would later be discharged, the Army citing alcoholism as their reason.

However, while stationed in Germany, Jeffery Dahmer reportedly abused one of his bunkmates, Billy Capshaw. It took

Capshaw twenty years of therapy before he was able to publicly speak out about it. Capshaw would later state that for thirteen months, Dahmer drugged, controlled, and tortured him. When Dahmer would leave the room, he would deny Capshaw the key. The room doors in the barracks locked from either side and without a key, Capshaw was effectively imprisoned in the room. His fellow soldiers wouldn't help him, and Capshaw jumped from a window, injuring his legs.

Dahmer would often leave Capshaw locked in the room for a full weekend while he stayed out. Left without food, Capshaw would resort to digging through Dahmer's belongings, searching for some, and would find bloody military knives, which he always threw out the window.

Many times, when Dahmer returned from his weekend away, he would be drenched with dried blood, so much that his clothes were glued to his skin.

There persists a very tangible theory that Jeffery Dahmer was, in fact, the abductor and murderer of six-year-old Adam Walsh. Upon Dahmer's dishonorable discharge from the Army, in March 1981, he made his way to Miami, where he planned to hide out to avoid his father's disapproving reaction. He had little money, and once it ran out, he camped out on the beach.

Eventually, Dahmer landed a job at a sub and pizza shop after the owner caught him rummaging for food in the dumpster outside. Dahmer appears in Florida records due to a police report in which Dahmer reported finding a dead body by the same dumpster on July 7, 1981.

Less than a week later, on July 13th, a ten-year-old boy would report a strange man chasing him and threatening to grab him in a Sears store inside a shopping mall just 50 miles north of Dahmer's workplace.

Witnesses would later describe the man to a police sketch artist. Another child's mother would also describe a man who tried to snatch her child in a Sears to sketch artists. The composite sketches bear a marked resemblance to Jeffery Dahmer.

When Adam Walsh was abducted in another Sears store inside a mall, his severed head would later be found 125 miles north of Dahmer's workplace. Witnesses would describe a blue van and a man throwing a protesting child into it. Witnesses who saw the man would identify him as Dahmer after Dahmer's arrest. The blue van, meanwhile, could have easily been the blue van for the pizza and sub restaurant Dahmer worked for.

After Dahmer's arrest, the FBI questioned him about the disappearance of Adam Walsh. Considering Dahmer was known to decapitate victims and had a record of indecency with children, it was a viable lead.

Dahmer denied any knowledge of the crime and was never officially linked to it.

In Dahmer's confession, he told police he didn't consider the skulls he kept to be trophies. He wanted to keep them because he felt the skulls represented the true essence of his victims. By keeping them, Dahmer stated, he felt like their lives weren't a total loss.

"Milwaukee Cannibal" Jeffrey Dahmer once admitted that his work as a chocolate factory mixer awakened homicidal and necrophilic urges he had otherwise suppressed.

After Dahmer's 1991 arrest, the public learned of the failure by the police to protect the naked and bleeding Konerak Sinthasomphone after one of Dahmer's neighbors called 911. The neighbor, who begged police not to return the boy to Dahmer, was threatened with arrest by police for interfering and being a nuisance. The police accepted Dahmer's story that the boy was his 19-year-old lover who was confused and upset, following an alcohol-fueled argument between the two.

Had police questioned any of these suspicious statements and ran a check on Dahmer, they would've discovered not only was he a registered sex offender, but his conviction also stemmed from molesting the brother of this same boy. It seems obvious that the police were anxious to be done with the situation, as evidenced by the conversation recorded as they checked back in with dispatch after the incident.

After assisting Dahmer with getting his victim back to the apartment, where he showed them Polaroids of the boy clothed only in underwear (to "prove" they were truly lovers), the officers laughed as they reported to dispatch it had only been a lovers' squabble between a couple of homosexuals.

Under fire, the department dismissed the officers, then quietly hired them back. Police never questioned the noxious odor of putrefying corpses in the apartment. Police didn't request Konerak be medically examined for injuries; in fact, they denied the boy was bleeding from his rectum, something several witnesses stated they'd noted. Had anyone done a physical exam on Konerak, it would've been difficult to miss the hole bored into his skull by Dahmer's hand drill and the blood coating his scalp.

Immediately after the police left, Dahmer murdered the boy and went on to claim five more victims before being arrested.

Dahmer's fellow soldiers were reportedly so frightened by his temper, especially when he had been drinking, that they would quietly ignore him getting drunk in the barracks while he lay in bed listening to his favorite metal bands on a Walkman.

After Dahmer was murdered in prison by a fellow inmate, two ex-soldiers who served with him in the Army came forward with claims he raped them during their military service, but they had been too embarrassed and frightened to come forward with charges while he was alive.

***

Dahmer was considered to be so dangerous that he remained shackled during his autopsy.

***

Jeffrey Dahmer made a sign for the wall inside his cell, which read: "CANNIBALS ANONYMOUS MEETING TONIGHT."

***

John Joseph Joubert IV's daydreams of murder grew and grew and, by the age of 12, he was enraptured with thoughts of strangling and stabbing boys, girls, and young women alike.

By age 13, he began physically tormenting his peers, stabbing and slashing young girls with any sharp object he had, severely injuring some.

He went on to kill three young boys between 1982 and 1983, at 18.

He was captured in 1984 and ultimately executed.

Jesse Pomeroy was the youngest person in Massachusetts convicted of murder. Between 1871 and 1872, a series of attacks occurred against young boys, in which they were lured to a secluded area before being beaten and stabbed by an older boy.

Pomeroy was arrested, charged, and found guilty of the attacks and sent to the State Reform School for Boys at Westborough when he was just thirteen.

In February 1874, he was paroled, but just one month later, a ten-year-old girl went missing. The following month, in April 1874, the body of a four-year-old boy was discovered at Dorchester Bay, leading to Pomeroy's arrest. The body of the 10-year-old girl was found in the basement of Pomeroy's mother's dressmaking shop.

Pomeroy was found guilty of the murder of the four-year-old on December 10, 1874. Eventually, he would also be found guilty of the murder of the little girl.

Pomeroy was sentenced to death, but his sentence was later commuted to life in prison. He served the majority of his sentence in the Massachusetts State Prison in Charlestown. In 1929, at 70 years old, he was transferred to Bridgewater Hospital. He died in the hospital three years later.

Harvey Robinson is known for being one of the youngest serial killers reported in the United States. At just 17 years old, Robinson attacked and raped five women, killing three of them.

One of his more brutal cases was when he broke into a home and raped and strangled a 5-year-old girl. She survived the attack.

Robinson was sentenced to death.

Although Harvey Robinson is known for being a young serial killer, Craig Price from Rhode Island was even younger.

An article in The Boston Globe put it:

"He stabbed four of his neighbors to death in their own homes before he was old enough to drive."

In 1987, when he was just 13, he stabbed Rebecca Spencer to death. Two years later, he killed Joan Heaton and her two daughters.

A minor at the time, Rhode Island law stated Price couldn't be tried and sentenced as an adult, meaning once reaching the age of twenty-one, he would be released. During his time in custody, however, he managed to rack up plenty of violations and wasn't due for release until 2017.

Before he could be released, he stabbed a fellow inmate, earning himself an additional twenty-five years.

Serial killer Robert Pickton fashioned a dildo to the barrel of a .22 caliber revolver to act as a makeshift silencer. People called him the "Killer Clown."

While it's true that John Wayne Gacy Jr. was both a killer and a clown, there's no evidence that he murdered any of his 33 victims while wearing a clown costume. Gacy dressed up as his alter egos, "Pogo" and "Patches," for parties, or sometimes to entertain children at nearby hospitals.

"When he was creepy and going to kill you was when he was dressed normally," says Rachael Penman, exhibits and events manager at the National Museum of Crime and Punishment.

When demolishing the house of serial killers Fred and Rosemary West, every brick was crushed and every timber beam was burned in order to discourage souvenir hunters.

When police in Ukraine captured Anatoly Onoprienko in 1996, he admitted to killing 52 people, mostly by shooting them. Onoprienko would select an isolated house and terrorize then kill everyone inside, be it by gun, axe, or hammer, and would then burn the house down, which resulted in the nickname "The Terminator."

Onoprienko was able to recount each disturbing detail of every murder he committed, and by all accounts, he was incredibly proud of what he had done. As a way to commemorate his dastardly crimes and to relive what he had done, Onoprienko kept the underwear that each of his victims wore when he killed them, even giving some of them to his girlfriend to wear.

After committing 43 murders in 6 months, he had amassed quite the collection of underwear.

On July 1, 1948, Charles Floyd broke into an apartment in Tulsa, Oklahoma. He attacked and raped a woman, as well as attacking her teenage daughters. He fled when a neighbor interrupted his assault.

Just down the street, Floyd cut a hole in the door of another home, entered, and bludgeoned the young woman inside to death. All of his victims that night had red hair.

Upon his arrest, Floyd confessed to police that redheaded women incited an overpowering lust in him. He also confessed that he had killed before.

Six years prior, Floyd killed the redheaded, pregnant wife of a fellow trucker. That same year, he raped and murdered a mother and daughter, both of whom were redheads. Two and a half years later, he killed a redhead he spotted undressing in her apartment.

Floyd was sent to a mental institution for life due to his low IQ.

Glen Edward Rodgers also seemed to have a thing for redheads. The "Cross Country Killer" traveled from state to state between 1993

and 1995. He'd cozy up to women and ask for favors. He even moved in with one, briefly.

He was convicted of five murders but bragged that he had murdered more than 70 people, including Nicole Brown Simpson. Four of his victims were women with reddish hair.

It turns out his mother was a redhead, and Roger's brother said that she had rejected and abused him.

Owing to the fact sibling serial killers are a rarity, as are female serial killers, one particularly interesting deadly duo was the Gonzalez Sisters.

During the 1950s and 60s, sisters Delfina and Maria de Jesus Gonzalez ran a huge prostitution ring in a small Mexican town near San Francisco. Known by the nickname *Las Poquianchis*, the sisters ran what one victim described as a combination concentration camp and brothel called, ironically, *Rancho El Ángel.*

To recruit new prostitutes, the sisters would regularly place job advertisements in the newspaper. Once the naïve victim accepted the fake job, they were taken forcibly to the sisters' ranch where they were tortured, sold into sexual slavery, and, often, in the end, murdered.

After being kidnapped by the sisters, most of the girls were force-fed drugs—an unfortunately-universal practice still commonly used. This is done not only to make the captives more compliant but also to intentionally create addicts. Addicts are much more pliant and willing to do the unthinkable to acquire the fix they so desperately need.

If any of the Gonzalez's women became sick, got pregnant, or lost attractiveness, they were murdered and buried in mass graves at Rancho El Angel. In 1964, three victims of the Gonzalez sisters escaped and alerted authorities to the crimes.

Searching the grounds of Rancho El Angel, authorities discovered the remains of 80 women, 11 men, and several fetuses. It was eventually revealed that the sisters were responsible for the deaths of many migrant workers and wealthy customers, in addition to their sex slaves.

The Gonzalez sisters briefly evaded police, but they were eventually captured and placed on trial for the murders. Found guilty of the crimes, the sisters were given forty-year sentences, much to the chagrin of the lynch mob assembled outside the building.

Delfina died in jail. Maria served her sentence and disappeared. Although also implicated in the sex crimes and murders, two additional Gonzalez sisters were never charged.

Lorenzo Gilyard, the "Kansas City Strangler," fell under suspicion of murder in 2004, nearly a decade after his last confirmed kill. Gilyard had begun murdering women in 1977, after escalating his crimes from rape, and killed his last confirmed victim in 1993.

Gilyard was linked to twelve murders, most of the victims being prostitutes, through DNA evidence. However, for several reasons, he was only convicted of six.

He was sentenced to life in prison without the possibility of parole, and police are still working to link him to the other six murders.

The FBI's *Serial Murder: Pathways for Investigations*, published in 2015, provided some new insight into an aspect of serial murder investigation many of us think little of.

A helpful guide for law enforcement personnel working unsolved serial murder investigations, and free to read on the FBI's website for any laymen interested, the book delves into research on the discovery of victims' bodies. The *"dump site"* generally being the first crime scene investigators encounter during the course of an investigation, how and where bodies were discovered can open insight into the killer.

The booklet states that body disposal scenarios can be classified in four ways: transported from murder site and concealed, transported from murder site and dumped, left *"as is"* at murder site, and left at murder site but concealed.

Body disposal methods can be used to uncover the nature of the crime, the relationship between victim and perpetrator, and the criminal experience of the murderer.

The only serial killer in the state of Delaware, the "Route 40 Killer," was apprehended on account of the only clue investigators had to go on: blue carpet fibers.

Between 1987 and 1988, prostitutes along Route 40 were picked up and murdered. Blue carpet fibers were found on many of the bodies.

An undercover officer hung out on Route 40 and was ultimately picked up by one Steven Brian Pennell in his electrician van. She immediately noticed the blue carpet covering the inside of his van.

Pennell was arrested and eventually found guilty of murdering two victims.

During his sentencing, despite not having confessed or admitting guilt, Pennell asked to be put to death. He was executed by lethal injection in 1992.

Most serial killers feel no compassion for others. It is why they are capable of committing atrocities to other people and "not feel a thing," as Charles Manson put it.

The mask of sanity, the pretending to be just the same as anyone else, was described by Henry Lee Lucas as being: *"like a movie-star... you're playing a part."*

Something to keep in mind when studying serial killers is that often their "reality" and perception of it isn't the same as "normal" people. That isn't to say they are, by the legal definition, "insane."

Most of us would never be able to murder a stranger, stash the body in our cellar, and entertain guests. But Canadian serial killers Paul Bernardo and Karla Homolka and Milwaukee's Jeffrey Dahmer did just that, even taking part in family dinners while their victims' bodies lay hidden in their respective cellars until they could be dismembered and disposed of.

Modus Operandi, or the method of operation in which a killer murders his victims, is a well-known attribute of a serial killer.

Another, equally important, aspect of a killer and his crimes is the posing of victims, though it is not a given occurrence in any serial killing. Some killers pose their victims' bodies wherever they have left them, or otherwise alter the crime scene. Sometimes, this is to throw investigators off by offering false, misleading clues, known as staging a crime scene. Other times, the posing of a body is an important part of the killer's signature and offers an insight into the killer's mindset. A killer could use the posing of the body to further his fantasy and give himself a sick satisfaction.

In the case of the Boston Strangler, victims were often posed with their genitals exposed toward the door to the room. The Strangler's sixth victim, 67-year-old Jane Sullivan, was left in the bathtub. She was knelt, her face in six inches of water, her bare buttocks exposed.

Investigators eventually concluded she was murdered elsewhere in the house, and her body was taken to the bathroom and posed.

William Lester Suff, the "Riverside Prostitute Killer," was convicted of killing thirteen women between 1988 and 1991. The majority of his victims were street prostitutes, and as a result, Suff left some of the bodies next to dumpsters with their arms turned outward to expose needle track marks. Such posing was a message regarding the worth of victims.

When Christine Smith was picked up by Robert Yates, her gut instinct immediately began going off. When Yates wasn't able to perform sexually, he snatched back the money he had given her and pulled out a gun. A struggle followed, and he shot at her head, but due to the confusion, the bullet only grazed her. She was able to escape and went to the hospital. She was treated for the wound, then went to inform police of her attack and give a description of her attacker.

After Smith was in a car accident, x-rays revealed she still had some of the bullet fragments in her skull. The fragments were extracted in hopes of matching them to bullets in other victims. This, combined with a bullet extracted from the roof of a car, led police to a .25 caliber gun once owned by Robert Yates.

Ted Bundy, Jeffrey Dahmer, and Sean Gillis were all heavy drinkers. Bundy was aware when the urge to attack women came on and knew drinking would remove the last vestige of humanity and inhibition so that he could carry out the gruesome acts. Dahmer drank to deal with his conscience and the memories of the things he had done. Gillis drank because he enjoyed being drunk.

A common denominator among many known serial killers is torment and animal abuse. It has long been thought these acts are a precursor of escalating violent acts, often leading to the taking of human life. On January 1, 2016, the FBI's National Incident-Based Reporting System (NIBRS) began collecting detailed data from participating law enforcement agencies on acts of animal cruelty, including gross neglect, torture, organized abuse, and sexual abuse. Before this year, crimes that involved animals were lumped into an "All Other Offenses" category in the FBI's Uniform Crime Reporting (UCR) Program's annual "Crime in the United States" report, a survey of crime data provided by about 18,000 city, county, state, tribal, and federal law enforcement agencies.

Conspiracy theories (or rumors) assert the J. D. Salinger novel *Catcher in the Rye* was found amongst the personal belongings of multiple would-be assassins and convicted killers, hinting that it was a kill trigger for those subjected to mind control experiments—in particular, the U.S. government's program du jour MK-ULTRA.

In his quest to become an infamous killer, Michael Gargiulo, charged with murdering three women, including a young lady which actor Ashton Kutcher was dating at the time of her death, studied books about his role model—Ted Bundy.

Joel Rifkin was arrested and found to be in possession of a dead prostitute. When a search warrant was executed on his property, a popular book about catching the Green River Killer was discovered. Rifkin later said in a television interview that reading the book was like reading a how-to book on serial murder.

Following the Bernice Worden murder trial of Ed Gein, presiding Judge Robert H. Gollmar would write:

> *"Due to prohibitive costs, Gein was tried for only one murder—that of Mrs. Worden. He also admitted to killing Mary Hogan."*

Although generally referred to as a serial killer, Ed Gein was only charged with one murder.

Over a decade after her murder, Gein was tried for the shooting death of Bernice Worden. He was found not guilty by reason of insanity.

Among the Ed Gein trophies authorities listed were:

- A wastebasket made of human skin.

- Human skin covering several chair seats.

- Skulls on his bedposts.

- Bowls made from human skulls.

- A corset made from a female torso skinned from shoulders to waist.

- Leggings made from human leg skin.

- Masks made from the skin of female heads.

- Mary Hogan's face mask in a paper bag.

- Mary Hogan's skull in a box.

- Bernice Worden's entire head in a burlap sack.

- Bernice Worden's heart "in a plastic bag in front of Gein's potbellied stove."

- Nine vulvas in a shoebox.

- A young girl's dress and "the vulvas of two females judged to be about fifteen years old."

- A belt made from female human nipples.

- Four noses.

- A pair of lips on a window shade drawstring.

- A lampshade made from the skin of a human face.

- Fingernails from female fingers.

By the time he was eleven, serial killer Derrick Todd Lee was torturing small animals and peeping in windows.

As a teen, Joel Rifkin was rejected by his peers and sought solace in books and films—about serial killers.

In 1980, while still a teenager, serial killer Scott Thomas Erskine beat a fourteen-year-old boy unconscious while attempting to rape him. Erskine was en route to a job interview for a camp counselor position at the time of the attack.

When the electric chair was introduced, it was meant to serve as a more humane form of execution, as opposed to hanging. Execution by electric chair was touted as a quick, painless death that occurred instantly upon the first jolt.

In reality, this was far from the truth. The first jolt was often never enough to kill the condemned, who usually writhed in agony as multiple jolts were given for several minutes. Often, during the course of this, the head of the prisoner in the chair would catch fire or bleeding would occur as the prisoner was slowly roasted to death.

Cary Stayner was 11 when his 7-year-old brother, Steven, was abducted by a pedophile and held captive for the next seven years.

In 1980, Steven freed himself and another child, 5-year-old Timmy White. The family and community were overjoyed that Steven was home and safe. All were rejoicing, except his brother Cary. Cary was eaten away by jealousy.

When Steven had disappeared, he was all the brothers' parents were able to talk about. To Cary, Steven was all they cared about. He felt unimportant, abandoned, and neglected. His jealousy gave way to anger as time passed, and, when his brother returned, the anger gave way to resentment.

Cary later told screenwriter J.P. Miller:

"His head was all bloated out... We never really got along well after he came back. All of a sudden Steve was getting all these gifts, getting all this clothing, getting all this attention. I guess I was jealous. I'm sure I was... I got put on the back burner, you might say."

Cary grew more and more withdrawn and began isolating himself.

Unfortunately, Steven died in a motorcycle accident when he was just 24.

By that time, Cary was spending most of his time in the mountains. He had lost all ambition and was working a dead-end job, living with his uncle, Jerry Stayner. This uncle was later found dead in his house from a shotgun blast to the chest. Cary had an alibi: he had been at work at the time.

In 1999, at 38, Cary began the killing spree he had dreamed of since before his brother vanished. He killed three young women in the Cedar Lodge motel he worked at near Yosemite Park.

Five months later, he murdered another woman.

He was apprehended soon after, and his mental instability was apparent. Cary gave reports of sexual abuse from the uncle who had so mysteriously been murdered.

He was ultimately sentenced to death. He finally became the center of attention he had strived to be for so long at his three-week murder trial.

Police Chief Tony Dossetti, who had rescued Cary's brother Steven, later said:

"It crossed my mind that maybe this was Cary's way of competing with his brother's notoriety."

Cary Stayner is still on death row.

Alfred Hitchcock's frenetic film *Rope*, in which we see Jimmy Stewart take a turn at solving the mystery, was based on the true story of the abduction and murder of 14-year-old Bobby Franks by Nathan Leopold and Richie Loeb.

In 1977, actor Peter Lorre's daughter Catharine was approached by two well-dressed men. Upon closer inspection, the duo noticed the resemblance to her father. Catharine confirmed Lorre was her father, and the men both expressed their admiration of him and walked away.

She thought nothing more of the incident until she saw mugshots of the men and learned they were charged with the "Hillside Strangler" murders.

The men were cousins Angelo Buono and Kenneth Bianchi. They confirmed Catharine's story. They were indeed big fans of her father's work.

Fan of old Hollywood movies? The 1942 classic, *Arsenic and Old Lace,* based on a play of the same name and starring Cary Grant, finds Grant panicking when he learns his elderly aunts are serial killers.

The crimes of serial killers Catherine May Wood and Gwendolyn Graham were the inspiration for the sisters Miranda and Bridget Jane in *American Horror Story: Roanoke.*

Chinese serial killer, Zhang Yongming, had an unbelievably gruesome M.O. Over the course of five years, he killed 11 young men he spotted walking near his home.

He would beat the men to death before scooping out their eyeballs. Though he fed some of their flesh to stray dogs, he sold the rest, labeled as "ostrich meat," at his local market.

When he was apprehended, police found a scene comparable to the Ed Gein crime scene. Bones hung from the ceiling in plastic bags, and various organs were either dried or preserved in bottles in order to make traditional "snake wine."

People with the condition called hybristophilia are actually aroused by serial killers. Numerous killers receive visitors in jail or even get married.

In extreme cases, hybristophiliacs will offer people they know as victims.

Dennis Rader is infamous for his long stretches between murders, as well as his love for taunting the police and press. He devised his own moniker when, ten months after his first murder, Rader wrote a letter to The Wichita Eagle paper signed: *"YOURS, TRULY GUILTILY."*

The letter included a post-script which read:

"The code words for me will be… Bind them, Torture them, Kill them, B.T.K., you see be at it again. They will be on the next victim."

His crimes spanned the decades between 1974 and 1991, with stretches between killings unlike investigators had seen before. The murders were often followed by communications to local media.

This weakness for taunting the press cost Rader his freedom and exposed him as the man behind the horrors in 2005.

On the 30th anniversary of his first murders, Rader teased the press with another letter, and in an unexpected chain of events, the letter was traced back to him.

After his arrest, he eventually confessed to all ten murders and was sentenced to 10 consecutive life sentences.

On April 11, 1896, infamous murderer H. H. Holmes wrote a grisly confession of all his crimes to the Philadelphia North American newspaper:

"I was born with the devil in me. I could not help the fact that I was a murderer, no more than the poet can help the inspiration to sing. I was born with the 'Evil One' standing as my sponsor beside the bed where I was ushered into the world, and he has been with me since."

One month later, he was hung at Moyamensing Prison.

Issei Sagawa's prison sentence for murder and cannibalism did not cause him to become a social pariah after release. In fact, just the opposite. He found himself in demand as talk shows vied to get him on their show.

He authored 20 books on his crimes, starred in a movie, and even found work as a—brace yourself—food critic.

Before he began murdering women, Peter Sutcliffe worked as a gravedigger. Seems a bit cart before the horse, doesn't it?

Looking back on her childhood, Mae West—daughter of convicted killers Fred and Rosemary West, not the film star of the same name—recalled that she and her sister, like most young girls, played dress-up with clothing they found in the house. They didn't know it at the time, but the clothes belonged to their parents' victims.

Scott William Cox was only convicted of the murders of two women, but he is believed by law enforcement to have committed up to 20 murders.

His job as a trucker took him far and wide across the Western half of the United States, which meant he could have very easily been considered as a suspect in even more crimes across that vast region.

He was working under an alias at the time of his arrest, and little is known about his background. He was paroled in 2013 and has since vanished. Maybe he is living under another name, or maybe he is a suspect in other, more recent, murders.

Italian serial killer Leonarda Cianciulli disposed of bodies by making them into bars of soap.

In 1896, serial killer Amelia Dyer was due to be executed when she was subpoenaed to give evidence in another trial. It was decided that her testimony would be inadmissible, as she was considered legally dead upon receiving her sentence.

BTK wrote,

"When this monster enter (sic) my brain, I will never know. But, it (sic) here to stay. Society can be thankfull (sic) that there are ways for people like me to relieve myself at time (sic) by daydreams of some victim being torture (sic) and being mine. It (sic) a big compicated (sic) game my friend of (sic) the monster play (sic) putting victims (sic)number down, follow them, checking up on them waiting in the dark, waiting, waiting. Maybe you can stop him. I can't. He has areadly (sic) chosen his next victim."

Convicted killer Ottis Toole and his partner Henry Lee Lucas made their reputation giving fantastical, sometimes blatantly unbelievable confessions to crimes they often had no way of committing. One or the other would confess to any crime presented to them, trying to outdo each other as though it was a competition.

Toole made national news after confessing to the notorious disappearance of six-year-old Adam Walsh. Walsh vanished from a shopping mall in Hollywood, Florida, while shopping with his mother on July 27, 1981. By the end of the week, his disappearance had made national headlines.

Two weeks later, a little boy's decapitated head, which matched the description of Adam Walsh, was found over 100 miles away. No leads or suspects were ever found, and the case began to grow cold until Ottis Toole confessed to the crime.

Toole would go on to confess 24 times to the Walsh murder, and even went so far as to write a letter to the Walsh family demanding $50,000 in return for the location of Adam's remains:

"Dear Walsh:

I'm the person who snatched, raped and murdered and cut up the little prick teaser, Adam Walsh, and dumped his smelly ass into the canal. You know the story but you don't know where his bones are, I do. Now you are a rich fucker, money you made from the dead body of that little kid. I want to make a deal with you… Here's my deal. You pay me money and I'll tell you where the bones are so you can get them buried all decent and Christian. I know you'll find a way to make sure I get the electric chair but at least I'll have money to spend before I burn. If you want the bones… you send a private lawyer with money for me. No cops, no State Attorneys. No FDLE (Florida Department of Law Enforcement). Just a private lawyer with a written contract. I get $5,000 as "good faith" money. Then when I show you some bones I get $45,000.

You get a lawyer to make up a paper like that. If you send the police after me before we make a deal then you don't get no bones and what's left... can rot... Now you want his tones (sic) or not? Tell the cops and you don't get shit. Sincerely, Ottis E. Toole"

John Walsh, Adam's father, didn't buy it.

Toole later recanted his confession and eventually died in prison of liver failure on September 15, 1996.

Lee Roy Martin killed four young women and girls between 1967 and 1968. After the final murder, he called Bill Gibbons, editor of the Gaffney Ledger newspaper in Martin's hometown, to report the locations of his last victim and two undiscovered bodies.

Martin advised Gibbons not to go check out the scenes himself and suggested he call the police to do so instead.

Later, Martin called Gibbons again and confessed to having murdered the first victim, for whose murder another man had been convicted. *"He's serving my time,"* Martin said.

He also told the editor, *"If they don't catch me, there'll be more deaths."*

Martin was arrested on February 16, 1968. He was sentenced to 4 life sentences.

He was killed by another inmate on May 31, 1972.

Juana Barraza, the "Little Old Lady Killer," was a former female wrestler infamously exposed as a serial killer. Barraza murdered at least 11 elderly women, entering their homes by helping carry their groceries or offering help with cleaning before brutally bludgeoning or strangling them.

Though she was charged with eleven murders, estimates by authorities and the press as to her victim count range from 24 to 49. Her victims were usually 60 or over and lived alone.

Oddly, Barraza's weapon of choice to strangle her victims was stethoscopes. Usually, she carried her own, though once she used one found at the scene of the crime.

She was eventually caught leaving the scene of a murder by her victim's lodger. She was sentenced to 759 years in prison in 2008.

Nannie Doss is perhaps one of the most infamous black widows in American history. A friendly, warm woman of 49 from Tulsa, Oklahoma, friends and neighbors were stunned when she confessed to having murdered the better part of her immediate family.

Four out of five husbands, two of her children, a grandson, her mother, her two sisters, and her mother-in-law had all been killed between 1920 and 1954 with arsenic. Doss was found out in October 1954, when her last husband, Samuel Doss, died in a hospital after having severe gastrointestinal distress.

When an autopsy was performed, arsenic was found in his organs, and Doss eventually confessed. She was sentenced to life in prison after pleading guilty to Samuel's murder on May 17, 1955. Despite her lengthy confession, she was only charged and tried for the death of Samuel.

"Jolly" Jane Toppan was a sadistic nurse who, in 1902, confessed to 31 murders. Her nursing career had a long list of unprofessional conduct, from thievery to manipulating patients' records to murder. Toppan murdered not only her patients but also her adoptive sister and some of her landlords.

Her weapon of choice was a combination of morphine and atropine. Once her patients were incapacitated, she would climb into their bed and fondle and kiss them as they died.

Toppan later reported, she wished *"to have killed more people—helpless people—than any other man or woman who had ever lived."*

Toppan was found not guilty by reason of insanity and sent to Taunton Insane Hospital, where she died in 1938, aged 84.

Between 1982 and 1988, a little old woman in Sacramento, California, drugged and suffocated at least nine of her boarders. Dorothea Puente, who had always had trouble with the law, earned herself the moniker "Death House Landlady" after her crimes were uncovered in 1988.

She killed between 9 and 15 of her boarders, all of whom were elderly or mentally disabled, and stole their social security checks. Seven bodies in total were found on her property, and she was arrested on November 11, 1988. She was charged with a total of nine counts of first-degree murder.

She was only convicted on three counts and sentenced to life in prison on December 11, 1993. Puente died in prison on March

27, 2011, aged 82, still insisting her victims had died of natural causes.

Sharon Kinne is a multiple murderer and remains on the run to this day.

It began in 1960, when her husband was found dead, shot in the head, with the couple's two-year-old daughter playing nearby. Kinne told the police that the two-year-old had accidentally shot him, as she was allowed to play with her father's guns. This could not be disproven, and the death ruled accidental.

Kinne had long been cheating on her husband and burning through his money, and her husband, James, had been considering divorce around the time of his death. Kinne received the life insurance payment, and she would have been in the clear if not for her next move.

About two months after her husband's death, in May 1960, Kinne killed the wife of one of her lovers, Patricia Jones. Jones' husband had ended his affair with Kinne, who was seeking to marry him. She confessed to Jones she was pregnant by him, but instead of wishing to divorce his wife, Jones merely cut ties with Kinne.

So, Kinne called Patricia at her office and told her that her husband was having an affair with Kinne's sister and asked to meet up to talk about it. Patricia disappeared later that day, and her body was eventually found in a secluded area that her husband and Kinne often went to on dates.

She had been shot, this time with a .22 pistol. Kinne was arrested on May 30 and released on bond on July 18.

Her trial was postponed long enough for her to give birth to her and Jones' daughter.

On June 21, 1961, Kinne was found not guilty of the murder of Patricia Jones, and on January 11 of the following year, Kinne was convicted of the murder of her husband. She was sentenced to life in prison and, before long, granted a new trial, which resulted in a mistrial, and so did the third trial.

After a fourth trial was scheduled, Kinne, on bond now, ran away to Mexico in 1964. It was here that she killed a man named Francisco Ordoñez with the same gun used to kill Patricia Jones.

She was arrested and sentenced to 10 to 13 years. However, she escaped the Mexican prison on December 7, 1969, and was never seen again.

Lavinia Fisher has garnered, by several researchers, the title as America's first female serial killer. Wife of John Fisher, the young couple were hanged for highway robbery in 1820.

Legend has it that the two operated an inn, and Lavinia would invite men to dinner, where she'd ask about their occupation to see if they were wealthy. In the legend, a fur trader named John Peoples once stayed the night at the Fisher's inn. During the night, a trapdoor sprung and Peoples, in his bed, was dropped into the cellar, where John Fisher waited with an axe. Peoples managed to escape, and the couple was arrested.

Sentenced to death, the story goes that Lavinia Fisher stepped to the gallows in her wedding dress.

In actuality, John Peoples was robbed by a gang of highwaymen, among whom were John and Lavinia Fisher, who stole $40 from him. The gang of thieves operated out of two inns in town, one of which they had burned to the ground following a dispute just before the robbery of John Peoples. When these inns were searched, two bodies, that had been there for some months, were found.

John and Lavinia Fisher were sentenced to death for the robbery and hanged.

Debra Brown chose the wrong man to get into a relationship with. Alton Coleman was on the run from the law when they met in 1984, facing charges of having sex with a 14-year-old girl.

Brown fell under Coleman's spell and broke things off with her then-fiancé, leaving her family to go on the run with Coleman. Together, the two committed rapes, assaults, and murders across six states in the Midwestern United States. In total, eight victims were murdered, usually by strangulation. Many of their victims were little girls under the age of 10, though they did kill several adults as well, including the mother of one nine-year-old victim and one 75-year-old man.

They also broke into homes, tied residents up, then assault and robbed them. Nearing the end of their crime spree, Coleman and Brown carjacked three separate people, kidnapping the first victim and killing the last.

They were arrested on July 20th, 1984, two months after their crime spree had begun. Both were sentenced to death, with

Coleman receiving an additional 100 years on other charges, and Brown receiving an additional 40.

Coleman was executed on April 26, 2002.

Brown escaped execution due to her low IQ, dependent personality, and nonviolent history. Her sentence was commuted to life in prison.

Judy Buenoano was convicted in 1984 for the drowning death of her handicapped 19-year-old son, Michael. The same year, she was convicted of attempting to murder her boyfriend.

Judy, born Judias Welty, had a hellacious upbringing, she would later state. After her mother's death, two-year-old Judy and her infant brother were sent to live with their grandparents, while her older siblings were put up for adoption. When her father remarried, Judy was brought back to live with them. Her father and stepmother reportedly abused her terribly, starving, beating, overworking her, and burning her with cigarettes. She snapped and attacked her family, spending two months in prison before being sent to a reformatory.

It was a year after leaving the reformatory in 1959 that she met her first husband, James Goodyear. Twenty-five years later, in 1985, she was charged with his murder. His body was exhumed after her son's death, and it was found to contain traces of arsenic.

For this, Judy Buenoano was sentenced to death. She was executed in Florida by electric chair on March 30th, 1998, earning a place as the first woman executed in Florida since 1848 and the third woman executed since the reinstatement of the death penalty in 1976.

Lyda Southard was Idaho's first confirmed female serial killer. Southard poisoned four husbands and at least one, but likely, two daughters, as well as her brother-in-law. From the deaths of these husbands, Southard raked in nearly $20,000 in life insurance.

A chemist and relative of her first husband named Earl Dooley was the first to truly take note of the odd circumstances in which so many people had died, all in some sort of gastrointestinal distress.

Upon exhuming the bodies of three of Southard's husbands, her youngest deceased daughter, and her brother-in-law, most of the bodies were found to contain arsenic, and the others had the appearance that they had once contained it.

Lyda was apprehended in Honolulu and extradited to Idaho. She was convicted of second-degree murder and sentenced to 10 years to life in prison but escaped in 1931, just after ten years incarcerated.

She married again, but her husband turned her in, and she was arrested in 1932.

Southard was released on parole nine years later and pardoned the following year, but charged with the death of a different husband.

Once more, she was sentenced to 10 years to life. She died of a heart attack on February 5th, 1958.

Rosemary West is certainly one of England's most notorious female serial killers. Alongside her husband, Fred West, she took part in the torture and murder of at least ten young women and girls, including her own daughter.

Her childhood was nightmarish, with a violent father who frequently sexually abused her. Her husband's childhood was also abusive. Rosemary's father continued to abuse her even after she married Fred.

Rose worked out of their home, now called the "House of Horrors," as a prostitute, often engaging with clients while Fred watched through a hole in the wall. These clients fathered three of her eight children, while Fred fathered the remaining five. Rosemary aided Fred in luring in young women and torturing them before eventually killing them.

Rosemary's crimes started when she murdered Fred's daughter by another woman in 1971. The pair's crimes began soon after, in 1973, and ended with the murder of their daughter, Heather, in 1987.

They were arrested in 1992, with Fred facing charges of sexual abuse against his daughter, and Rosemary charged with child cruelty. During the investigation, the disappearance of Heather came to light.

Ultimately, Fred would be charged with 11 counts of murder, and Rosemary with 10.

Fred committed suicide before their trial. Rosemary was eventually convicted and sentenced to life in prison on November 22, 1995.

The first African American female serial killer in the United States was Clementine Barnabet. Between 1909 and 1912, she invaded homes in Texas and Louisiana and killed entire families with an ax.

The most prolific female serial killer in history, Elizabeth Bathory, sexually abused, tortured, and killed over 600 young women.

The most prolific female serial killer in history, Elizabeth Bathory, sexually abused, tortured, and killed over 600 young women.

Serial killer Rodney Alcala acted as his own attorney in his trial. For 5 hours, he interrogated himself on the witness stand, asking questions addressed to "Mr. Alcala" in a deep voice and answering them in his normal voice.

The Cabinet of Dr. Caligari, a 1920 silent film, is regarded as the first serial killer movie. The plot centers around the idea that a person can be hypnotized and turned into a killing machine.

Decades later, the CIA's MK Ultra program would come to light, in which LSD and mind-control were experimented with in hopes of creating a super-soldier.

The movie *Deranged*, released in 1974, follows the story of Ezra Cobb and his Gein-like obsession with his mother. He embarks on a killing spree, collecting corpses to keep his mother's corpse company.

Cruising, a film released in 1980, follows the story of a police officer, played by Al Pacino, who goes undercover in New York's gay scene to catch a serial killer preying on men.

Almost a decade before directing *A Christmas Story*, Bob Clark directed another holiday movie, this time with a twist. The holiday slasher flick *Black Christmas* brought Clark the credit of being the first person to use in a movie the classic phrase, *"The calls are coming from inside the house."*

1969's *The Honeymoon Killers* tells the story of real-life killer couple Martha Beck and Ray Fernandez, in the low-budget, yet gruesome, film directed by Leonard Kastle.

By day, Vlado Taneski of Macedonia was a journalist and crime reporter. By night, however, he was a serial killer. He went so far as to report on his own crimes, which would be his downfall after he reported details only the killer would know.

Jack Unterweger did the same thing, reporting on crimes he committed at the time he was committing them.

After his crimes were discovered, serial killer Marcel Petiot grew a beard and joined the police using the alias "Captain Valeri." Under this new guise, he was assigned to track down Petiot, until months later when someone recognized him.

By the age of 24, Richard Speck had been arrested more than 41 times, was addicted to drugs and alcohol, and sported a "born to raise hell" tattoo, lest anyone doubt his commitment to hellraising.

Speck's wife, whom he had impregnated when she was only 15, said he would rape her at knifepoint—often multiple times a day.

His parole officer at the time had this to say:

"When Speck is drinking, he will fight or threaten anybody. As long as he has a knife or gun. When he's sober or unarmed, he couldn't face down a mouse."

Dennis Nilsen gained infamy after his arrest in 1983 uncovered a string of murders from 1978 to that year. Nilsen, by the end of it, claimed the lives of 15 young men, keeping their bodies in his apartment before eventually dissecting them and disposing of their remains in the garden behind his apartment building.

Nilsen's mother, Betty Scott, never turned her back on her son, though she did admit his guilt to herself. She wrote him countless letters over many years, but he never replied. She wished nothing more than to see him and ask him why he'd killed those men.

"I would like to speak to him to see why he did this," she said in an interview with a Scottish television show. *"He was just nothing like he turned out to be... He never fought at school. He was never nasty to anybody."*

Joanna Dennehy made headlines in England after going on a 10-day killing spree in 2013. She stabbed five men, three of whom she knew, and two chosen at random.

When asked why she had done it, she merely replied:

"I killed to see how I would feel, to see if I was as cold as I thought I was, then it got more-ish."

Dennehy's mother was shocked when the news of her daughter's murder spree broke. She couldn't believe her daughter had been capable of killing anyone.

In an interview, she said:

"The girl that killed those people is not my daughter. My daughter's that nice 16-year-old that never came home... She was

very sensitive. If she stood on a worm or something she would be really upset if it died—she used to take them to bed with her. So, she was a loving girl."

Richard Ramirez's father, Julian Ramirez, expressed surprise and disappointment at his son's actions. He also blamed his son's drug use:

> *"I believe the marijuana he's been smoking put him out of control... In my heart, I can't believe he would have arrived at that. But if the authorities there have proof, what can we do?"*

Ted Bundy saved a toddler from drowning, apprehended a purse snatcher, and was appointed assistant director of Seattle's Crime Prevention Advisory Commission prior to his first confirmed murder.

While at the Wichita courthouse to get his City Inspector Badge, Dennis Rader was given a tour of the war room for the serial killer "BTK."

Years later, it was uncovered that he was, in fact, "BTK."

At the time of his execution in 2014, Tommy Lynn Sells was suspected of killing at least 70 people. He stated that his first kill was at age 16 when he killed a man he caught molesting a young boy. If true, it is ironic that Sells himself then went on to abduct, rape, and kill minors, including the 13-year-old whose murder got him the death penalty.

William Devin Howell boasted to his cellmate about his "garden," where he buried a string of victims who had all gone missing in 2003. He was known to speak of his "murder mobile," a 1985 Ford Econoline which had gotten him caught after the blood of a dead young woman, Nilsa Arizmendi, was found inside it.

In this same car, it was alleged, he slept next to the body of at least one victim. In 2007, three bodies were found behind a Connecticut strip mall. In 2015, an additional four sets of remains were found.

Authorities believe William Howell was responsible for all the deaths. Howell pled guilty to manslaughter in the case of Nilsa Arizmendi and is currently serving out a 15-year sentence.

The electric chair was introduced in New York in June 1888. The first person to be executed by electric chair was William Kemmler, who murdered his mistress during a fight, on August 6, 1890.

Not only was Dennis Rader working for ADT installing home security systems, he sometimes let himself in a potential victim's home and napped in their beds while waiting for them to get home.

Adolfo Constanzo was taken by his mother as a baby to be blessed by a Palo Mayombe practitioner. He would grow up to become a priest in the religion, sacrificing people in the belief that the ritual would protect his drug deals and other illegal activities.

Anthony Sowell was arrested in 2009 after police discovered the bodies of 11 women in his home. Sowell was nicknamed the "Cleveland Strangler," as all of his victims died from strangulation.

Three years after Sowell's arrest, a new serial killer from the same city would begin killing women in the same manner as Sowell, inspired by his crimes.

Gina DeJesus had no reason not to trust her friend's father, or so she thought. He was a familiar face, and he worked as a school bus driver. That fateful day, Gina had planned to have a sleepover with her friend, Arlene Castro, but Arlene's mother said no.

Gina walked home from school alone, then accepted a ride from Arlene's father, Ariel Castro. Castro abducted Gina, keeping her captive alongside other women, chained up in his basement for ten years, subjecting her to torture and rape.

Castro maintained a normal appearance, even going so far as to attend vigils for Gina.

The longest prison term handed down was 141,078 years in Bangkok. The crime? Not murder—it was given to a businessman for "swindling the public."

Herbert Mullin tried to "prevent an earthquake" by killing more than a dozen victims.

By the end of his teenage years, Bruno Lüdke had already murdered, raped, and committed necrophilia on a number of women. Born in 1909, Lüdke was rounded up during Adolf Hitler's genocidal rampage, labeled as a "mental defective," and sent to be experimented on.

However, during the course of the experimentation, Lüdke managed to strangle and stab 85 women before he was ultimately killed during an experiment gone wrong on April 8, 1944.

Though John Paul Knowles was called the "Casanova Killer" by the press, novelist Kurt Vonnegut Jr.'s daughter compared the serial killer, whom she met before anyone learned he was a serial killer, to Charles Manson.

In August 1987, Harrison "Marty" Graham found himself evicted from his apartment after a noxious smell emanating from it got too much to bear. When police investigated, they found the bodies of seven women, ranging in decomposition from fresh to skeletal.

Upon initial questioning, Graham insisted the bodies were there when he moved in. Eventually, he admitted that he'd "accidentally" strangled the women during sex.

Graham was heartbroken to lose his favorite possession after his arrest. It was a stuffed Cookie Monster doll that he took everywhere with him and even had conversations with. Graham was crushed when it was kept as evidence, and he was no longer allowed to sleep with it.

John Wayne Gacy claimed not to recall the incident that occurred when he was six years old. Allegedly, he stole most of his mother's underwear and took it to his special play area under the porch. This was the beginning of a lasting trend. Six or seven years later, after a similar incident, Gacy's mother punished him by making him wear the women's underwear. A couple of years later, his sister found even more women's underwear stashed in his bed.

Jerry Brudos' hallmark foot fetish began when, as a little boy, he found a discarded pair of women's heels at the local dump. When he brought them home, his mother berated him and forced him to discard them. He didn't obey, and when she found them later, she made him watch as she threw them in a fire. Unwittingly, she turned the shoes into a taboo that lured Brudos in more and more the older he got.

The first victim of the "San Francisco Witch Killers" was 23-year-old Keryn Barnes, their roommate. Suzan Carson later claimed that, while hiking home in the rain with husband and partner-in-crime, Michael Carson, she received psychic orders from God to kill Keryn.

The realization dawned on Suzan that Keryn had not been a psychic prophet like herself, but a witch hell-bent on destroying her and Michael all along.

Suzan later explained in her confession that Keryn was a "psychic vampire witch" who had blocked Suzan's own psychic abilities while leeching away her beauty and powers.

Spouses of both Robert Lee Yates and Gary Ridgway thought their husbands were having affairs, but never imagined they were out committing murder.

Rumor has it that a three-year-old boy in the Middle East claimed to remember dying in a past life. He told elders in the community he had been killed with an ax and led them to the bones and the murder weapon.

He next decided to confront the man who had killed his former self. The man was shaken but only confessed after the bones and ax were recovered.

The ax wound on the skull perfectly corresponded to a red birthmark on the little boy's head.

Police ruled the death of 33-year-old Nadine Haag a suicide. Her body was found in the shower in her apartment in Sydney, Australia, in December 2009, with one wrist slit. To support the suicide theory, a suicide note was found in her handwriting, but her family didn't buy it.

Haag had been involved in a grueling custody battle with her notoriously violent ex-boyfriend, Nastore Guizzon. Her family had suspicions that he had killed her and staged it as a suicide. And there were plenty of facts to back it up.

The cut on her wrist was nearly to the bone, which was excessively deep for a suicide and tricky to do on oneself. Pills were missing from a bottle, as though she'd taken a handful, but no traces were found in her system.

Behind her suicide note was a scrap of paper that read, *"He did it."* But police had failed to notice it. Even further, those same chilling words were found scratched into the bathroom tile by the new tenants.

In 2013, the coroner disagreed with the ruling of suicide, but there was not enough evidence to place Guizzon at the apartment on the day of the murder.

Kenneth McDuff, a Texas serial killer, was on Death Row, then pardoned and paroled, committed more murders, was re-arrested, and finally executed.

His case caused an overhaul of the Texas Justice system, including harsher sentencing, more prisons, and a rise in executions.

In 1996, infamous serial killer "The Yorkshire Ripper," Peter Sutcliffe, was almost strangled to death in custody before being saved by serial killer Kenneth Erskine aka "The Stockwell Strangler."

Sondra London, an American true crime author, earned herself a controversial reputation. The one-time girlfriend of murderer G.J. Schaefer and fiancée of serial killer Danny Rolling used her intimacy with both killers to pick their minds about their crimes and motives, then published the results.

The crimes of Charles Starkweather and Caril Ann Fugate have been immortalized in the movies *Badlands* and *Natural Born Killers*. The young couple went on a short but devastating killing spree, leaving 11 dead in their wake.

The first murder occurred on November 30th, 1957, when a gas station attendant refused to sell the couple a stuffed toy Fugate wanted. Starkweather shot the attendant, Robert Colvert, then robbed the gas station and stole what money he found on Colvert.

On January 21, 1958, Starkweather massacred Fugate's family. Her parents disapproved of him and his troublemaker reputation. Adding to their disapproval was the fact that Starkweather was 19 and Caril just 14. That fateful night, Fugate's parents warned Starkweather yet again to stay away from their daughter. Enraged, Starkweather shot them to death, then stabbed and strangled Caril's two-year-old sister.

When Caril Fugate came home, she helped Starkweather hide the bodies before the two hid out in the house for a week, denying visitors. Fugate's grandmother grew suspicious and threatened to call the police, so the young couple went on the run, robbing a house and stealing the car.

Abandoning the first stolen car, the two hitched a ride with a couple, who was later found shot to death in a storm shelter. They broke into another house and shot the couple living there, and stabbed their maid.

One final victim was killed on January 29, 1958, when he found Fugate and Starkweather sleeping in his car. The couple shot him. Shortly after speeding off, a police officer began to tail them.

Eventually, Starkweather surrendered. He would be sentenced to die in the electric chair, and at Caril's trial, he stated:

"If I fry in the electric chair, she should be sitting in my lap."

Starkweather was executed on January 25, 1959.

Fugate was sentenced to life in prison, although she was paroled in 1976.

Henry Lee Lucas used to dump his victims' bodies on the stretch of highway between Odessa, Texas, and Gainesville, Florida. Cops nicknamed it the "Henry Lee Lucas Memorial Highway."

While incarcerated at Statesville Prison, a video surfaced of Richard Speck and a second unidentified inmate. In the video, Speck is wearing ladies' underwear and very little else. On full display is a pair of extremely large breasts. It was clear Speck had been taking female hormones—which he readily admitted.

While Speck panders to the camera, his "friend" snorts cocaine from various locations on Speck's body, and the two engage in sex acts. Speck tells the unseen camera operator—presumably another inmate—how easy it is to get drugs or other contraband in Statesville.

In a portion of the film, the killer flashes several hundred-dollar bills and remarks:

"If they only knew how much fun I was having in here, they would turn me loose."

The video sparked outrage and became one of the driving forces for prison reform in America.

Robert Berdella was callous in a way many can't imagine. He recorded each word his kidnapped male captives spoke after waking up bound and then subjected to endless torture.

Berdella carefully wrote down the chemical or drug he gave, as well as the amount, injection site, time given, and victim's response. Just as methodically, he recorded the date each man eventually died from the torture. Everything he recorded would be used to torment his other victims.

Arnfinn Nesset was a bit of an anomaly. It is not often one hears about Norwegian serial killers, and the quiet nursing home worker did not seem to have the qualities that one associates with serial killers. Nevertheless, Nesset, who had been able to procure large quantities of the neurotoxin curare, began killing in 1977 and says he is not certain of his total number of victims.

Charged with 22 murders but thought to have killed more than 100, Nesset himself said:

"I've killed so many, I'm unable to remember them all!"

He went on trial in 1983 and was found guilty of embezzling funds from nursing home residents and guilty of the 22 murders he was charged with.

His sentence? Twenty-one years—not even one year for each of his known victims.

Michael Madison, a convicted rapist, murdered Shirellda Terry, Angela Deskins, and Shetisha Sheeley, whose bodies were all found in his neighborhood in 2013, wrapped in garbage bags.

All three women had been subjected to torture, mutilated, and strangled, and at least one had been raped. Madison was arrested and confessed to the crimes, though he showed no remorse.

In court, he smirked at and taunted the victims' families.

One victim's father, Van Terry, couldn't take the provoking any longer. From the witness stand, Terry looked to Madison and said:

"I guess we are supposed to find it in our hearts to forgive this clown."

Madison smirked yet again, and Terry was outraged, lunging across the courtroom to attack Madison.

Madison was sentenced to death for the murders.

As a teenager, Jerry Brudos stalked women and lunged at them, attacking them, and stealing their shoes. Things escalated quickly from there with Brudos—by seventeen, he had begun working on a cave in which to keep his captive sex slaves.

Kenneth McDuff managed to dodge three death sentences and was paroled in 1989. He is widely believed to have killed a woman just three days after his release.

Within no time, he was returned to prison for violating his parole by making death threats. He was released again on December 18, 1990, and seemed to lay low for about a year before killing again in 1991. By 1992, five more women were dead.

He was eventually arrested and sentenced to death after a coworker recognized him on America's Most Wanted.

Sean Vincent Gillis, over the course of a decade, killed eight women in the Baton Rouge area, shocking local law enforcement with the depravity of his crimes. His victims were raped, strangled, stabbed, and mutilated—sometimes dismembered, sometimes partially eaten.

Sean Gillis considered himself to be in a personal competition with Baton Rouge serial killer Derrick Todd Lee, who was convicted of two murders and suspected of at least five additional deaths.

Like Gary Ridgway's and Dennis Rader's spouses, Sean Gillis' wife never suspected she was married to a serial killer. Although there were periods of time Gillis would be gone that couldn't be accounted for, his wife maintained she thought he was merely having an affair and didn't confront him with her allegations.

Sean Gillis left the body of his first victim under a "dead end" road sign as a twisted joke.

Sean Gillis developed a pattern of strangling his victim with a zip tie before raping and dismembering them.

After his trial and conviction, Sean Gillis' wife continued to live in the house where her husband dismembered and cannibalized women.

Over the course of approximately a year and a half, Earle Nelson raped and strangled to death at least 20 women, most of whom were running boarding houses during the Great Depression to make ends meet.

Ted Bundy was a man with many fetishes. Voyeurism, pornography, bondage, rape, murder, necrophilia—and feet.

"This is for real. I mean, I've got a sock fetish. No question about it. I must have six or seven pairs right here with me in my cell. I am really sick when it comes to socks. These are some of the things for people who really want to know what makes Ted Bundy tick. They're parts of the combination to the deepest, most secret recesses of my mind. I'm very close to my feet. Right now. I'm lying on my back with my foot propped up on the bars. And I'm studying my toes. For a good portion of the night. They're probably the most attractive feet you've ever seen. Socks are such a serious part of my

life. They're so very important to me. They kept reading the list of socks and all and I felt proud. Honestly, it didn't even begin to occur to me that people might wonder why I had all these socks. I just felt proud that I owned all those socks. The only time I began to have a little bout of sheepishness was when he read about a white sock with a blue band and green stripe on the toe. Those are odor eaters—and that was getting too personal."

This statement provided a glimpse into the psyche of a true sociopath. He wasn't embarrassed or sheepish about the criminal acts he committed. He didn't say his actions were sickening. Instead, these feelings are ascribed to his fondness of objects because he is incapable of most feelings and emotions one normally has for another person.

For a year and a half, Henry Lee Lucas and many law enforcement officials claimed he was the most prodigious killer in history, with as many as 3,000 victims.

Then *Dallas Times Herald* reporter Hugh Aynesworth started sniffing around and rooted out the implausibility of Lucas's claims. If anything, it hurt Lucas's feelings to be called a liar—until

Aynesworth explained to Lucas that he was going to be executed for crimes he did not commit.

In the process of trying to catch serial killer Andrei Chikatilo, Soviet police inadvertently solved more than 1,000 unrelated crimes, including 95 murders and 245 rapes.

After the capture of serial child killer Robert Black, a police officer at the scene found his own daughter tied and gagged in the back of the killer's van.

When Kala Brown and her boyfriend, Charles Carver, went missing on August 31, 2016, many believed they had run away together. Others, however, suspected foul play.

Several months went by before authorities discovered a badly beaten Kala chained up like a dog on the property of convicted sex offender Todd Kohlhepp. Kala had witnessed the love of her life get shot in the head before she was chained up and shoved into a shipping container.

This container was her residence for three months, and she only saw the light of day when Kohlhepp took her outside for walks.

Police had received a tip to search Kohlhepp's property and discovered Kala as she frantically screamed from inside her prison. Kala was rescued, and a search of the property revealed two buried bodies.

Kohlhepp was also discovered to be responsible for a quadruple murder in South Carolina.

When Richard Ramirez broke into 16-year-old Whitney Bennet's home on July 5, 1986, it was a divine intervention that saved her life. Ramirez brutally beat her with a tire iron before pulling out a telephone cord to strangle her with.

As he squeezed tighter, sparks began flying, and Ramirez took it as a sign from God that Whitney was not meant to die that day. He fled the scene, leaving Bennett alive.

Tracy Edwards thought nothing of accompanying a man home from a bar on July 22, 1991. However, once he arrived at the apartment, he felt noticeably uneasy. The whole place had a strange odor wafting through it, and barrels littered the rooms. The man was acting strangely, too.

He quickly secured a handcuff on Tracy's wrist but was unsuccessful in securing the other. As the two watched a movie, the man lay his head on Tracy's chest, and as if it was the most normal thing to say in this situation, told Tracy he was going to cut out his heart and eat it.

Tracy kept his cool, playing along with the man in hopes of survival. He kept him talking, hoping to stall him long enough to stay alive. When he got the chance, Tracy punched the man in the face, knocking him backward, and bolted out of the apartment. With one handcuff dangling from his wrist, Tracy reported the man to the police.

When the police arrived, they discovered the remains of 17 bodies scattered throughout the apartment.

The man arrested was identified as Jeffrey Dahmer.

Cynthia Vigil Jaramillo believed she was under arrest as the man placed handcuffs on her and told her she was in trouble for solicitation. However, this man was not a police officer. Instead, he was a sexual sadist by the name of David Parker Ray. He took Jaramillo back to his trailer, which was full of torture devices.

Ray and his accomplice, Cindy Hendy, tortured and raped Cynthia for three days. Throughout it all, Cynthia remained alert, looking for any chance to escape. She finally received her chance when Ray left her in the care of Hendy.

Cynthia waited until Hendy was distracted and grabbed a key nearby, freeing herself from her chains. Then, she smashed a lamp over Hendy's head and ran out of the trailer. Battered, bloodied, and wearing only a dog collar, Cynthia was able to find help and report her abductors to the police.

David Parker Ray would earn himself the moniker "The Toy-Box Killer" and would be suspected of killing 40-60 victims. Though no bodies were found, he was sentenced to 224 years in prison for the abduction and torture of three women.

He died from a heart attack less than a year after his sentencing.

Cindy Hendy, meanwhile, received 36 years for her part in the crimes.

On September 3, 1986, Wayne Nance broke into the home of Doug and Kris Wells, planning to murder both. Nance stabbed Doug and left him to die in the basement, while he forced Kris into the bedroom and sexually assaulted her. However, Doug was still alive. He staggered up the stairs and grabbed a gun, making his way into the bedroom where he confronted Nance.

During the ensuing struggle, Doug knocked Nance down and shot him in the head, killing him.

Police were able to link Nance to at least five murders from the 1970s and 80s.

Sean Cribbin had a casual sexual encounter with Bruce McArthur in the summer of 2017. The encounter had ended with Cribbin unconscious, but he hadn't reported it to the police.

The day after McArthur was discovered to be a serial killer, Sean received a call from police about the unlucky encounter. Sean wasn't sure how they had found out until they asked if he'd noticed any cameras inside McArthur's apartment.

"I didn't remember any cameras, but as the [interview] was winding down, I knew at this point there were photos of me. [They] said to me that I was bound. I was in pretty much, for lack of a better term... a kill position. It hadn't dawned on me until we got further along in the conversation how much danger I was in that day and how close I was to not coming back," he said.

Charisma Carpenter is an actress known for her roles in *Buffy the Vampire Slayer* and *Angel*, but a story from her past became the basis for a true crime show, *Surviving Evil*.

Carpenter had kept quiet about the story for two decades. When she was 22, she had been out with a couple of male friends when all three were held at gunpoint by an attacker. It was 1991, and Carpenter was a cheerleader for the San Diego Chargers.

The attacker was a serial rapist, who also happened to be a San Diego police officer, by the name of Henry Hubbard Jr. He shot both her friends after a struggle, seriously wounding them.

Somehow, Hubbard was shot in the hand and fled the scene.

He was later implicated through his flashlight, which had been used in numerous other attacks prior. Hubbard is currently serving a 56-year sentence.

In 2011, Rhonda Stapley went public with the horrifying story she kept a secret for 37 years. It happened when she was 21 and attending the University of Utah, where she accepted a ride from a handsome stranger.

He introduced himself as Ted as she climbed into his Volkswagen Beetle. Ted took Rhonda to a remote canyon area, where he would rape her while choking her. Ted would allow Rhonda to slip in and out of consciousness during the attack.

She eventually escaped, throwing herself into the nearby stream, which carried her away. She ended up back in civilization but told no one about that night.

A year later, during his first arrest, Rhonda realized the man who had assaulted her was none other than Ted Bundy. She felt guilty for not having reported him. Maybe lives could have been spared.

In 2011, she shared her story with fellow survivors on anonymous online forums and detailed her experience in a journal. When she showed the journal to true crime author Ann Rule, Rule encouraged her to write a book about it.

Dennis Rader made his mark on Wichita, Kansas, during his decades-long killing career as "BTK." He was notoriously patient, going for years between kills and abandoning a victim he'd staked out if the conditions weren't right. Many people whose homes had been broken into were worried they had been targeted, and after his 2005 arrest, some wrote to him to ask if they had been.

One survivor had definitely stuck out in Rader's mind. Her name was Anna Williams. On April 28, 1979, Rader waited, sitting in her home, for her to arrive home from square dancing. But she never showed. Instead, she had stopped by her daughter's house for a visit.

Rader grew tired of waiting and left. He wanted her to know she had missed him. He sent her a taunting 19-line poem titled: *"Oh, Anna, Why Didn't You Appear?"*

Margaret Palm was abducted in 1981. Her kidnapper was already on the run from the police, wanted for the murder of Carrie Marie Scott. His murder spree had lasted for a decade at this point, as he'd made it his routine to jump from state to state, living under fake names and flying under the radar. He had earned the moniker "The Chameleon."

His name was Stephen Morin. He drove with Margaret Palm for ten hours, and Palm eventually convinced Morin to listen to tapes of a Texas evangelist, Reverend Kenneth Copeland. She also read him her journal of Bible verses.

This gave Morin a change of heart, and he let her go. She later stated he was on his way to turn himself in to Reverend Copeland when he was arrested at a bus stop.

Morin would be executed in 1985 for three murders and named as a suspect in over 30 more across the country.

Maria Hernandez pulled into the garage of her home on March 17, 1985. It was here that the 29-year-old would have the most horrific encounter of her life. As she stepped out of the car, she heard a noise. She turned to see a man creeping up on her, pointing a gun in her face.

She was unaware that this man was Richard Ramirez, who would terrorize Los Angeles during the following months as "The Night Stalker." Ramirez fired the gun as Maria put her hands over her face.

Her attacker made his way into the condominium where her roommate, Dayle Okazaki, was.

Maria survived; the bullet bounced off the keys she was clutching in her hand. Her roommate, however, would not. Maria ran and hid behind a car.

When Ramirez exited the building, he wanted to shoot her again, but changed his mind and made a quick escape.

Maria rushed inside to check on Okazaki, but he was already dead.

A year later, Maria came face-to-face with Ramirez again, this time in court as she testified against him.

Felicity Nightingale narrowly escaped Fred West and his House of Horrors. It was 1980, and Felicity had a habit of hitchhiking between her Weymouth home and the Welsh village where she had a summer job.

It was a cloudy afternoon when a friendly truck driver dropped her off at a service station on the M5 motorway. Felicity, on the hunt for her next ride, was approached by a man who offered her a lift. She immediately got bad vibes from the man, especially when he insisted that she throw her bag in the back instead of allowing her to keep it with her up front.

He went inside the station for a cup of tea, insisting Felicity join him. She went along with it, rather naïvely, and accepted his offer of a ride.

While driving, the man told Felicity she probably wouldn't make it home before dark and offered to let her stay with him and his family in Tewkesbury. She politely declined, but he brought it up again a bit later, claiming they were going the wrong way for her home in Weymouth, but they would need to pass through Tewkesbury.

Felicity knew they were going the right way to get to her home, as she'd traveled this road countless times, but her driver had such

265

a volatile temper that she kept quiet about it. Eventually, the man announced he had to pay a visit to a friend nearby and dropped her off in the middle of the roadway, telling her to cross over to the other side, and he'd swing back by to pick her up.

Felicity was just glad to be out of the van. Where she was at, however, she knew the chances of finding another ride would be slim, but she decided to wage her bets. Luckily, she found another ride that took her back to the service station.

It wasn't until 14 years later that Felicity recognized the strange man who picked her up that afternoon as Fred West.

Lisa McVey Noland brought down serial rapist and murderer Bobby Joe Long with her keen wits. The 17-year-old girl was biking home from work one November morning in Tampa Bay in 1984. Suddenly, Long pulled up beside her and yanked her off her bike. He tied her up and threw her in his car.

Long took Lisa to an apartment, where he raped her for the next 26 hours. Lisa had actually planned to kill herself upon returning home, having written her suicide note the night before. She had suffered years of sexual abuse from a family member and couldn't take it anymore. Now in immediate danger, Lisa had a change of heart and made it her mission to fight to save her own life.

Lisa had seen many crime shows and what she'd gleaned from those helped her, as did her wits.

When Long calmed down, Lisa later said she talked to him *"like a four-year-old"* in hopes of humanizing herself in his eyes and thus making it harder for him to kill her. It worked.

When Long was done with her, he dropped Lisa off in her neighborhood.

She had made mental notes of the details of him, his car, and the apartment, which resulted in police apprehending Bobby Joe Long.

It was the 1980s. Roger Sproston left his home in the West Midlands to hitchhike across America. He eventually got a job in Los Angeles driving an ice cream truck, but when the truck ended up stolen, he was out of luck.

When Sproston decided to hitch a ride downtown, he was approached by a man driving a red Ford Pinto. He didn't feel threatened by the driver, per se, but felt the man was giving off a bad vibe. Something wasn't quite right, but nothing was wrong enough for Sproston not to jump in the Pinto.

Unluckily for Sproston, the driver was infamous serial killer William Bonin, one of three serial killers prowling the Southern California highways during this decade. As Bonin drove, he started mumbling under his breath. That was enough for Sproston, who asked Bonin to pull over and let him out. Bonin pulled the car over on the side of the freeway, seemingly obliging Sproston's request.

Immediately, however, he pulled out a length of cord and wrapped it around Sproston's neck, attempting to choke him. Sproston had managed to slip his fingers under the cord before Bonin tightened it. He turned around and kicked Bonin in the groin, then tumbled out of the car. Bonin sped away.

Sproston flagged down a police car and gave them his story. He learned, much to his surprise, that police were already looking for several people killing hitchhikers on the highways.

Sproston gave a description of Bonin and his car, and just ten days later, William Bonin was in custody.

On September 13, 2016, a 911 call came to law enforcement in Ashland, Ohio.

"I've been kidnapped," the woman, identified later only as "Jane Doe" per state laws, whispered.

Though distressed, the woman did her best to remain calm as she explained softly that she was trying not to wake up her abductor, who slept nearby armed with a Taser. She had tried to escape, she said, but all the doors in the weather-beaten house were either locked or had no doorknobs.

She was able to give the authorities the address of the house, and officers arrived shortly to rescue her before her abductor woke up. The house was nightmarish and filthy.

Under a pile of clothes, police found the strangled body of a woman. In the basement lay a decomposing body of another.

Jane Doe explained that she had been held inside the hell house for days, tied up, and repeatedly raped. Police arrested her abductor, a man named Shawn Grate.

He calmly confessed to the murders of the two dead women in his house, as well as three additional murders. He claimed that he was never going to kill Jane Doe. Instead, he insisted, the two were going to get married.

He was eventually convicted of five counts of murder in three separate trials, as well as the sexual assault and kidnapping of Jane Doe. He received two life sentences and one death sentence.

Kate Moir, seventeen, was abducted by Australian killer couple David and Catherine Birnie in 1986. They had already abducted, raped, and murdered four women within the last month. They abducted Moir at knifepoint and took her back to their home in Perth.

Upon arrival, she was tortured and repeatedly raped. She was handcuffed to David and made to sleep in the bed that night. The following day, David left for work. Meanwhile, Catherine had forgotten to chain up Kate when she went to the door for a drug buy.

Kate managed to escape through a window. Upon her arrival at the police station, Kate found it hard to get anyone to believe her story. A 22-year-old rookie officer, Laura Hancock, was assigned to Kate's case.

Hancock believed Kate due to the level of detail and specifics Kate was able to provide. The young girl explained that while she was being held, the couple played a *Rocky* VHS tape and a Dire Straits cassette, that she discovered David Birnie's real name on a medicine bottle, and described little drawings she made around the house to convince others she had been there. These details got police to investigate.

Eventually, the Birnies were arrested, and David confessed to four murders and led police to the bodies.

On July 2, 2005, an eight-year-old girl would bring to light the vicious serial killer who had abducted her and her brother. On May 16 of that year, law enforcement discovered the bodies of Brenda Groene, her 13-year-old son Slade, and her fiancé, Mark McKenzie, viciously slain in their Idaho home. Immediate concern rose when it was noted that Brenda's youngest children, 9-year-old Dylan and 8-year-old Shasta, were missing.

An Amber alert was sent out, and the FBI began a massive search, but no leads arose for seven weeks. The case broke when, in the early morning hours of July 2ⁿᵈ, four patrons at a Denny's restaurant spotted a little girl who they recognized as the missing Shasta Groene they'd seen on the news. The patrons called the police, and the man with Shasta, Joseph Duncan, was arrested.

Shasta was reunited with her family, but authorities had little hope they would find her brother alive. They asked the public for tips, namely those about sightings of the car Duncan was driving during the seven weeks since the children's abduction. These tips led to the discovery of the body of Dylan Groene in a remote campsite on July 4ᵗʰ.

Most of the details about the case were uncovered during interviews with Shasta. Shasta gave the police a full account, beginning from when Duncan killed her mother, brother, and mother's fiancé. She stated that Duncan abducted her and Dylan in a stolen jeep and moved them to different remote campsites for nearly two months, repeatedly molesting them. During these moves, Dylan was killed.

Duncan pled guilty to multiple counts of murder, kidnapping, and sexual assault. He also confessed to the 1997 murder of 9-year-old Anthony Martinez—which earned him a life sentence in California—and the 1996 murders of sisters Sammiejo White, 11, and Carmen Cubias, 9.

In total, Duncan received nine life sentences and three death sentences.

Steven Stayner was seven when he was offered the car ride on December 4, 1972, that would change his life forever.

The car, driven by sex offender Kenneth Parnell, pulled up beside Steven as he made his way home from school. Steven accepted the ride. He would not be seen again by his family for eight years.

During his first week being held by Parnell, Steven was told Parnell had been given legal custody of him, and his name was now Dennis Parnell. Steven would later report that, during his captivity, Parnell sexually assaulted him 700 times.

Parnell would confess that the number was far higher. Parnell moved Steven a total of 12 times, enrolling him in various schools, some of which had even been given missing posters with Steven's name and picture.

Steven began drinking alcohol in middle school. Once he hit puberty, Parnell began searching for a new, younger child to abduct. He convinced a friend of Steven's to lure in 5-year-old Timmy White. Timmy White was abducted on February 14, 1980.

Steven knew he couldn't let Timmy suffer as he had, and on March 1st, while Parnell was away working a night shift, Steven and Timmy escaped and hitchhiked to the police station.

Parnell was arrested the next day for both kidnappings. Prosecutors would not charge him with the sexual assaults against Steven, believing it was in Steven's benefit not to mention it due to the stigma surrounding male sexual abuse.

Parnell was sentenced to seven years in prison for the kidnappings but paroled after serving five.

Due to the case, California lawmakers would change the laws and allow kidnapping sentences to run consecutively.

Steven found it difficult to adjust to a stable, abuse-free, and alcohol-free home life but eventually adjusted well. He would go on to give interviews for the book: *I Know My Name is Steven*, as would Parnell.

Steven grew into a well-rounded, kind young man who spoke out on ways to protect children. He married in 1985 and had two children. Sadly, his life was cut short at 24 when he was killed in a motorcycle accident on September 6, 1989.

More than 500 people attended his funeral, and Timmy White, then 14, helped carry his coffin.

Timmy would go on to become a Los Angeles Sheriff's Deputy. He would later say he had a nice time with Steven during their time together, reading comic books.

Timmy died on April 1, 2010, of a pulmonary embolism, at just 35.

Kenneth Parnell, meanwhile, was arrested again on January 3, 2003. Then 72, Parnell attempted to convince his caretaker to buy a 4-year-old boy for him. He was sentenced to 24 years in prison for attempting to buy a child and attempted child molestation.

He died in prison on January 21, 2008.

The FBI reported that of the 500 "known" serial killers, 16% of these were adopted. The percentage of adopted peoples in the general population being only 2-3% means this is an abnormally high number.

William Heirens spent over six decades in prison for murders many people believe he did not commit.

In 2019, 22 death row prisoners were executed in the United States. As of October 2019, there were 2,639 inmates waiting on Death Row.

The Collector, a 1963 novel by John Fowles made into a movie by the same name, sparked a fire inside monstrous serial killers Leonard Lake and Charles Ng.

The story centered around a man who must resist his fantasies of abducting and turning his victim into his personal sex slave. He kidnaps a woman named Miranda, locks her away, and treats her as nothing more than an object.

Leonard Lake and Charles Ng were enraptured by the story, which fed into their own similar desires. The two built an underground bunker and began abducting women, often snatching them from the safety of their own homes and killing any witnesses, even their children.

They would hide away the women inside the confines of their bunker, filming themselves in a makeshift studio as they tortured and killed their victims. Lake kept a video diary in which he divulged his desires for a perfectly submissive *"on the shelf"* woman to serve his every desire and be readily available but otherwise keep out of sight. Those who did not comply with these desires were raped and killed. He called this the "Miranda Project," an homage to *The Collector*, which was found in the bunker.

Bonding with your baby is one of the most precious moments in a parent's and a child's lives. But if an infant doesn't get the attachment it needs, there could be stark results.

"It's so difficult when you bring a child with RAD into the home because there's such little knowledge of the problem," Charlie Brown, advocate for RAD treatment, said.

RAD is short for Reactive Attachment Disorder, a rare condition that can lead to severe psychological issues.

"The worst case of those are the kids who become gang members, serial killers," Brown said. *"They're the ones when there's a school shooting it's a RAD kid."*

Serial killers Jeffrey Dahmer and Ted Bundy were diagnosed with the rare mental illness. Symptoms include low self-esteem, lack of self-control, aggression and violence, and lack of empathy/compassion/remorse.

"When they have no attachment to others, they don't develop a conscience. They truly don't care what you feel or think," Brown said.

If you were to carefully calibrate your fear of being murdered according to statistics, you should be 12 times as afraid of your family members than of serial killers.

Less than one percent of murders in any given year are committed by serial killers, according to the Federal Bureau of Investigation's report on serial murder.

In 2012, 12.5 percent of murders were committed by victims' family members.

Based on the Radford University serial killer database, which includes data on nearly 4,000 killers, just 46 percent of serial killers since 1910 have been white men.

In his book *Why We Love Serial Killers*, Dr. Scott Bonn discusses an experiment he performed to discover if misconceptions and fear of serial killers are perpetuated mainly from the media. He looked at articles mentioning serial killers in *The New York Times* and *Time* magazine between 1995 and 2013, and searched within them for the words *"devil," "monster,"* and *"evil."* In both publications, 35 percent of articles contained one or more of those descriptors.

Around 8:15 on the morning of July 15, 1997, world-renowned fashion designer Gianni Versace returned to his Miami Beach home from a walk to a nearby café. A man approached Versace and pulled out a gun, killing him with two shots to the back of the head.

The gunman ran, tailed by a witness, and disappeared inside a parking garage. Inside the parking garage was a red pickup truck linked to a murder in New Jersey. The owner of the truck was Andrew Phillip Cunanan, the subject of an ongoing manhunt.

Cunanan was a 27-year-old Californian college dropout who, for some time, engaged in relationships with various sugar daddies.

Out of the blue, in April 1997, he began a killing spree. His first target was a former naval officer he bludgeoned to death, and a few days later, he shot an architect, dumping both men's bodies near East Rush Lake in Minnesota. Both men were long-term associates.

Come May, Cunanan killed an elderly stranger in Chicago and stole his car, driving it to New Jersey, where he murdered another man. He stole that man's car and drove to Miami.

By now, the pieces were beginning to fall together, and Cunanan was connected to each seemingly random murder.

The FBI joined in on the hunt, and various gay communities across the country were on the lookout for Cunanan, with the New York City Gay and Lesbian Anti-Violence Project even putting up a large reward for his capture.

Cunanan made the FBI's Ten Most Wanted list in June 1997. However, he managed to stay under the radar until the murder of Gianni Versace. Eight days later, the caretaker of a houseboat just two miles from Versace's house reported hearing a gunshot. It was Cunanan.

Responders to the scene found him dead from a self-inflicted gunshot wound.

Though his rampage had ended, he would never be able to tell what exactly triggered it all.

There have been countless new technologies designed to help capture serial killers, beginning most notably with the FBI's Violent Criminal Apprehension Program (ViCAP). However, ViCAP never became widely used due to the 189 (later cut to 95) questions that investigators would have to answer and input into the program each time.

In 1991, an incredible leap was made when Kim Rossmo, a Vancouver policeman turned professor of criminal justice, devised a new algorithm to predict where a serial killer might live. The algorithm used the various locations of victims' bodies when compared to where identified suspects live.

In 1992, Michael Aamodt, professor of psychology at Radford University, created the Radford Serial Killer Database, which compiled the demographic information of over 4,500 serial killers.

In 2015 came another innovative step when journalist-turned-sleuth Thomas Hargrove devised the Murder Accountability Project (MAP). Hargrove's MAP used an algorithm that accounted for the style, place, time of killings, and demographic information about the victims, which could be used to hone-in on potential killers.

Clarence Elkins took the path to justice himself when the legal system wouldn't. In 1998, he had been convicted of the murder of his mother-in-law and the assault of his six-year-old niece.

Despite proof that the DNA found did not match him, he was denied an appeal. Clarence's wife was his biggest supporter, working overtime to get him exonerated. She began an investigation of her own and found a likely suspect who was in the same jail as her husband.

Clarence collected the suspect's discarded cigarette, and DNA left on it was found to match that in the 1998 crime.

The prosecutor still refused to overturn the conviction, but the attorney general publicly shamed him into doing so. After Clarence was released, it was uncovered that the real killer was a convicted sex offender who lived next door to the victims. To boot, the killer had once asked a police officer why they hadn't arrested him for the murder yet.

Grover Thompson died in prison while serving a 40-year-sentence for a crime he didn't commit. After the 1981 attempted murder of Ida White, 72, in Mount Vernon, Illinois, Thompson was arrested. He was 46, and his health deteriorated quickly in prison.

Just 12 years after his arrest, Thompson was confined to a wheelchair. He died in 1996.

A decade later, in 2007, serial killer Timothy Krajcir confessed to former Illinois police officer Paul Echols that he had, in fact, been the one to stab Ida White.

Thompson was posthumously pardoned, the first man convicted of such a crime to be posthumously pardoned in Illinois.

Texas serial killer Carol Cole endured teasing from his classmates for having a "girl's name." He drowned one of those tormentors at the age of 10.

Until Cole's admission decades later, the death was thought to be an accident.

In the middle of the murder spree that would end up taking 13 lives, Richard Ramirez was nearly arrested by a police officer named John Stavros. But Stavros let him go. Stavros had caught Ramirez racing through a red light in a stolen car, flying away from the scene of a crime where a woman had just escaped being abducted by a man who fit Ramirez's description.

"Hey," Stavros said, slowly piecing together that he might be looking a serial killer in the eye. *"You're not that guy killing people in their homes, are you?"*

It was a masterful stroke of police work—the beginning of an interrogation that we swear we are quoting word for word.

Ramirez said that he wasn't, and for a moment, the officer was satisfied. Stavros was willing to suspect that this man had killed and raped multiple women, but he wasn't about to call him a liar.

Still, a distinct possibility seems to have dawned on Stavros: What if Ramirez was the Night Stalker, and he'd just forgotten?

"You... sure you're not him?" Stavros asked.

Ramirez kindly reassured him. *"Hey, man, it's not me."*

Perhaps Stavros should have been a little suspicious when Ramirez started praying to Satan and scratching a pentagram into the hood of his stolen car. Perhaps Stavros should have done a little more to stop Ramirez when he leaped over a fence and ran away.

And maybe if Stavros had reported all this to the other police officers, they would have found the mountain of evidence that was inside the car Ramirez left behind—evidence that, when they did find it, ended up cracking the case.

Ramirez, though, had promised he wasn't a serial killer. It just wouldn't be right not to take him at his word.

Gary Heidnik kidnapped six women between November 25, 1986, and March 23, 1987. Locked in his basement for the duration, many outsiders and even police had no idea the women were there until one escaped and dialed 911.

It came as no surprise to the family of one woman, Sandra Lindsay. Sandra was the second woman to be abducted by Heidnik, and her family contacted the police. They even suspected Gary Heidnik had been the one to abduct Sandra. However, Julius Armstrong, the detective assigned to the case, dismissed their suspicions. He tried to discourage them from searching for their daughter, saying:

"Why are you worried about your daughter? She's 25."

Sandra's parents insisted and finally pressured him enough to get him to go to Heidnik's house. Armstrong did the minimum.

"I knocked on the door," he reported. *"I didn't receive any answer. I left a message for anyone known as Gary to contact West Detectives."*

Heidnik didn't make contact, and Armstrong didn't press it further.

"In my mind," he said after the news broke of Heidnik's involvement. *"This person was missing voluntarily."*

286

The women were left to save themselves. By the time they freed themselves, Sandra Lindsay was already dead. The night she died, police visited Heidnik's house again following complaints of a strange odor coming from the residence. They accepted Heidnik's explanation that he had merely burnt his cooking.

It would eventually be revealed that the smell had come from Sandra Lindsay's dismembered body roasting inside Heidnik's stove.

When reports came out of a mysterious man attacking and raping women around Scarborough, Canada, Alex and Van Smirnis had little doubt as to who the man could be.

They knew one man creepy and perverse enough to commit such crimes: their childhood friend, Paul Bernardo. They called numerous times to offer Bernardo's name to the police. When police called Paul Bernardo in, they interrogated him and took DNA samples from him.

Those DNA samples were sent off to the forensic department for testing, but the forensic department never followed through. They still didn't follow through when Paul Bernardo's fiancée's 15-

year-old sister died just 33 days later. Nor did they when it was revealed the girl, Tammy Homolka, had been drugged, raped, and died by asphyxiating on her own vomit, or when it was noted that Paul had lied and said he called an ambulance immediately. He had waited twenty minutes, covering up evidence with the help of his fiancée, Karla Homolka.

Bernardo's DNA still went untested when the Smirnis brothers repeatedly called the police and tried to convince them Bernardo was behind these crimes.

It would be two-and-a-half years before the samples were ever tested, and by then, Bernardo had killed three teenage girls.

Between June 2014 and September 2015, the bodies of four men were dumped in a graveyard right around the corner from Stephen Port's house.

Benjamin Cohen, CEO of LGBT news site *PinkNews*, noticed this connection and asked police to see if there was a link. All four men had died of an overdose of the date-rape drug GHB just after arranging dates on Grinder and were then found dumped in the same spot.

Police insisted it was just a coincidence that gay men kept dying of a drug overdose in the same graveyard and warned Cohen not to publish anything. After all, he wouldn't want to get people scared over nothing, right?

Police continued to deflect suspicions of foul play until the sisters of one victim, Jack Taylor, took the case into their own hands. The sisters reviewed CCTV footage of Taylor going into the graveyard with an unknown man. Police had seen this footage but didn't care to investigate it before Taylor's sisters insisted.

Upon investigation, the man was revealed to be Stephen Port, who was arrested two days later.

<hr />

Albert Pierrepoint, who presided over 400 hangings in England between 1932 and 1956—including the Nazis tried at Nuremberg—was considered England's most prolific hangman as well as its most humane.

In his 1974 memoir, *Executioner: Pierrepoint*, the then 69-year-old ex-executioner disavowed the death penalty as a plausible deterrent.

Robert Pickton was exposed as a horrendous serial murderer after police obtained a warrant to search his Port Coquitlam, British Columbia, Canada, pig farm for illegal fireworks.

Pickton was taken into custody on February 6, 2002, while police obtained court orders to search the farm for the B.C. Missing Women Investigation. During their search, they found numerous personal items belonging to the missing women.

Pickton was initially charged with 26 counts of murder, though that was eventually dropped to 6.

On December 9, 2007, Pickton was found guilty on all six counts and sentenced to life in prison with no chance of parole for 25 years.

In 1974, Ricardo Caputo was released from a mental institution where he had been committed after being deemed incompetent to stand trial for the 1971 murder of a woman in Long Island. Just days after Caputo's release, his psychiatrist was found dead in her apartment in Yonkers.

Caputo spent 20 years on the run, assuming numerous identities, abandoning a wife and children, committing two additional murders, moving to Latin America and back to the United States, and, near the end, settling down with a new wife and children and working as an English teacher.

In the last year of being on the run, Caputo claimed he began to remember his crimes and feared the return of a homicidal alternate personality. He flew from Argentina to New York City, where he turned himself in to the police and confessed to killing his psychiatrist, a woman in Mexico City, and another woman in San Francisco.

At only 11 years old, Mary Flora Bell was convicted of murdering two young boys during the summer of 1968.

Florida Judge Edward Cowart was known for his Southern rhetoric in the courtroom, combining good old Southern morals and sensibilities with kindness and compassion, and for quoting the Bible while pronouncing a firm, but fair, sentence on those who stood before him.

One of the speeches he gave to a man standing before him, found guilty of multiple murders, was so poignant that once heard, is not easily forgotten.

The deeply moving words even made their way to Hollywood, becoming the title of a biographical movie about the man in Cowart's courtroom.

Extremely Wicked, Shockingly Evil and Vile is the title of the 2019 biopic about serial murderer Ted Bundy, but that is only part of the speech. Here it is, in its entirety:

> *"The court finds that both of these killings were indeed heinous, atrocious and cruel. And that they were extremely wicked, shockingly evil, vile and the product of a design to inflict a high degree of pain and utter indifference to human life. This court, independent of, but in agreement with the advisory sentence rendered by the jury does hereby impose the death penalty upon the defendant Theodore Robert Bundy. It is further ordered that on such scheduled date that you'll be put to death by a current of electricity, sufficient to cause your immediate death, and such current of electricity shall continue to pass through your body until you are dead.*

"Take care of yourself, young man. I say that to you sincerely; take care of yourself. It is an utter tragedy for this court to see such a total waste of humanity, I think, as I've experienced in this courtroom.

"You're a bright young man. You'd have made a good lawyer and I would have loved to have you practice in front of me, but you went another way, partner. I don't feel any animosity toward you. I want you to know that. Take care of yourself."

— Judge Edward Cowart

In some places, it is still customary to charge a bullet fee for prisoners executed by a designated shooter or firing squad. A bullet fee is a charge levied to the family of executed prisoners to reimburse the prison or local authorities for the ammunition used to execute the condemned. Bullet fees have been levied in Iran, as well as in China.

In 1990, three forensic experts gathered for lunch, and their discussion turned to the solving of cold cases: William L. Fleisher, a former Philadelphia Police Officer and FBI agent was then

Philadelphia's second-in-command U.S. Customs Special Agent; Frank Bender, a well-known forensic sculptor from Philadelphia; and Richard Walter, a prison psychologist from Michigan.

The trio wanted to establish a venue where like-minded persons, both in and outside the field of forensics, could gather to discuss and debate crimes and mysteries.

The Vidocq Society was born, named for Eugène François Vidocq (1775-1857), the criminal-turned-detective who founded the French Sûreté and is considered to have been the first modern detective.

In Texas, you don't have to commit murder to get the death penalty. Texas statute books still provide the death penalty for aggravated sexual assault committed by an offender previously convicted of the same against a child under 14.

Billy Moseley's headless and handless body was discovered in 1974. Three years later, Reginald Dudley and Robert Maynard were charged with the murder and convicted.

A few months later, in 1977, Billy Moseley's head was discovered in a public toilet. Rumors at the time indicated Dudley and Maynard had someone place the head there to cast doubt on their guilt—but who? And where had Billy Moseley's head been hiding?

For three years, from 1873 to 1876, a caped figure struck terror in the hearts of citizens in Boston, Massachusetts. Over the course of three years, at least five women and girls were murdered, and scores were raped by a man wearing a black cape.

The mysterious figure was, at last, caught after he was observed taking a young girl into a church. The girl's ravaged body lay lifeless where her attacker, Thomas Piper, left it.

Piper was taken into custody. He confessed. He was executed on May 26, 1876.

In 1943, 16-year-old Jo Ann Kiger awoke from a nightmare that she was being attacked by a monster who was intent on murdering her family. The nightmare did not end when she awoke.

The teen realized she held a shotgun in her hands and had shot her father, brother, and mother. Both Jo Ann's father and younger brother lay dead, her mother injured, but alive.

At trial, the girl's mother testified her daughter had been a sleepwalker her entire life.

On May 14, 1973, Billy Isaacs, his brother, half-brother, and a friend murdered a family of five in their home in Georgia.

Only 16 at the time of the murders, Isaacs served as a witness for the prosecution, ensuring he would not receive the same sentence handed down to the three older boys—death.

Liu Yongbiao's literary career ended when it was discovered his art actually did imitate life. The 53-year-old writer told police who came to arrest him at his home in 2017 that he had been waiting for them for two decades.

In 1995, Yongbiao and a friend were guests in a hostel. Before the night was over, they murdered the owners and two others, including a 13-year-old boy.

In the preface to his 2010 novel, *"The Guilty Secret,"* the Chinese author expressed his desire to write a suspense-filled detective story about an alluring female writer who dodges arrest despite committing a string of murders.

"I came up with the idea after reading some detective novels and watching crime shows and movies," Mr. Liu wrote at the time. *"The working title is: 'The Beautiful Writer Who Killed.'"*

By the 1880s, a general grumbling issued forth from Buffalo, New York's citizens, regarding the execution of prisoners by hanging. The New York Times in 1882 alone ran 50 articles graphically detailing the sights, sounds, smells, and agonies of the condemned as they struggled against their earthly bonds.

Few people then, or now, know what event helped pave the way for research into a more humane way of executing prisoners.

In 1881, a man named George Smith, known to be a heavy drinker, made his way to a local power plant, where workers heard him loudly proclaim that he was going to stop the generator. Upon grasping the machinery, Smith promptly dropped dead. Everyone in the vicinity attested to the fact Smith looked uninjured and had given no sign nor sound of distress.

During the postmortem exam, doctors were intrigued by the absence of burns or scorch marks on Smith's corpse. A local dentist, Dr. Alfred Porter Southwick, was fascinated by the report and teamed up with a fellow physician, Dr. George Fell, to conduct experiments.

With the support of the SPCA (Society for the Prevention of Cruelty to Animals), the two began endeavors to calculate the amount of electricity needed to humanely put down animals. After months of trials—and many errors—the doctors were satisfied with their results, which they published in many scientific journals.

It was not long before Dr. Southwick was proposing electrocution as the most humane way of executing criminals. In 1888, the Electric Chair Bill was passed, and two years later, New York state executed the first prisoner, William Kemmler, by electrocution.

One of America's most well-known ballet dancers, Jacques d'Amboise, forged a successful career as a performer and choreographer both on stage and in Hollywood musicals. While attending ballet school in California during his teen years, d'Amboise stayed at the home of a Pasadena couple and became friends with their son, William Bradford Bishop Jr.

By 1976, Bishop had a job with the U.S. State Department and lived in Bethesda, Maryland, with his wife, three sons, and elderly mother. On February 29 of that year, d'Amboise had a performance scheduled at the Kennedy Center, and both he and his wife were planning to stay in Bethesda with the Bishop family. However, two days before the show, d'Amboise suffered a knee injury and was forced to cancel his performance. As a result, his scheduled stay at the Bishops' home never happened.

One week later, d'Amboise was shocked to learn that the burned bodies of William Bradford Bishop's wife, children, and mother were all found in a shallow grave in North Carolina. The last time anyone saw Bishop was the day of the murders.

Frustrated over not getting a promotion he felt was owed to him, he left work early on March 1, 1976. He returned home that night and bludgeoned his entire family to death before driving their bodies to North Carolina.

To this day, William Bradford Bishop has not been found and remains one of America's most wanted fugitives.

On August 15, 1995, after continually disrupting court proceedings, murderer Christopher Charles Lightsey was gagged during the sentencing phase of his trial for the killing of William Compton, a 76-year-old cancer patient.

He stabbed Compton 42 times and stole his gun collection, a jar of coins, and other items.

The killer, also a suspect in the 1990 murder of a 4-year-old girl, was sentenced to death and currently spends his time on California's Death Row.

On August 4, 1967, 15-year-old James Gordon Wolcott grabbed a .22 long-barrel rifle and killed his father, mother, and 17-year-old sister in cold blood.

When police arrived at the scene, they found the only survivor, Wolcott, behaving hysterically.

At first, no one knew for certain whether the teen survived the massacre by good fortune or by his own design. While being questioned by police, Wolcott broke down and admitted to being the shooter.

He was charged with the murders, booked into the county jail, and his trial began a couple of months later. His defense lawyer stated he had a pre-existing mental condition exacerbated by the teen's habit of sniffing model glue. A court-ordered psychological examination confirmed Wolcott's diagnosis of paranoid schizophrenia. The only reason he gave for committing the murders was simply that he hated his family.

After a trial lasting six months, Wolcott was found not guilty by reason of insanity, and he spent the next six years in a mental hospital. After his release, Wolcott changed his name and disappeared.

Almost four decades passed before anyone heard from him. It turns out, after changing his name, he went on to earn a Ph.D. in psychology, later joining the teaching staff of Millikin College in Decatur, Illinois. During his three decades of service, he was the recipient of the college's Teaching Excellence and Leadership Award.

Wolcott, now Dr. James St. James, was soon offered the position of chairman for the Behavioral Sciences department. After learning about the professor's dark past, local officials, including the mayor of Decatur, were calling for his removal, but the college stood by Dr. St James, who is still the chair of Millikin's Behavioral Science Department, and his experimental psychology classes continue to receive excellent reviews on social media.

Haunting last words:

"Turn up the radio and I'll go quietly."

—Peter Manuel

"I am the master of my fate. I am the captain of my soul."

—Timothy McVeigh

"Good people are always so sure they're right."

—Barbara Graham

"Capital punishment: them without the capital get the punishment."

—John Spenkelink

"I can't really pinpoint where it started, what happened, but really believe that's just the bottom line, what happened to me was in California. I was in their reformatory schools and penitentiary, but ah, they create monsters in there."

—David Long

"Mindy, I'm with you, honey. I do not know why, Mindy, you are doing this, but I will still forgive you. You know he is a murderer. Why don't you support me? He will do it again. Mindy, you are lucky you are still alive."

—Jerry Lee Hogue

III

Trivia Quiz

1. Serial killers generally stalk and kill their prey in three ways. Which one of the following is not one of those ways?

    a. Nomadic

    b. Direct

    c. Territorial

    d. Stationary

2. Which serial killer purportedly sent the following message to a local newspaper:

"Sir I send you half the Kidne [sic] I took from one woman prasarved [sic] it for you tother [sic] piece I fried ate was very nise [sic] I may send you the bloody knif [sic] that took it out if you only wait a whil [sic] longer."?

   a. Jeffrey Dahmer

   b. Jack the Stripper

   c. Ed Gein

   d. Jack the Ripper

3. Which serial killer professed his innocence by declaring his victims all sent him telepathic messages that they were willing sacrifices and ready to die?

   a. William George Bonin

   b. Herbert Mullin

   c. Randy Kraft

d. William Ray Pugh

4. True or False: The label "Bad Seed" used to refer to serial killers' personalities is derived from William March's 1954 novel of the same title.

True

False

5. Which of the following statements about American serial killer Albert Fish is not true?

   a. A prison x-ray revealed at least 29 needles in his pelvic region.

   b. Albert Fish's real name was Hamilton Fish.

   c. A New York jury found him insane and sentenced him to life in a mental institution.

d. Authorities compiled a list of 18 separate types of paraphilia practiced by Fish, including coprophagia—consumption of human excrement.

6. Which of these murderers was at one time an employee of contractor and serial killer John Gacy?

   a. Edward Spreitzer

   b. Thomas Kokoraleis

   c. Andrew Kokoraleis

   d. Robin Gecht

7. What name did the murderer in the previous question give to his group of murderous friends?

   a. Satan's Slayers

   b. The Demented Demons

   c. Lucifer's Left Hand

d. The Ripper Crew

8. True or False: Studies show that only 30% of all serial murders are sexually motivated.

True

False

9. This serial killer blames the disappointment in his birth mother once they met with being part of the catalyst for his crimes.

10. This serial killer entertained young males and murdered them in the family home while his wife and children were away visiting his in-laws.

Bonus: What was the family's home in the previous question called?

11. The female half of one serial killing duo shared the same name as the wife of another infamous serial killer. What was the name shared by both women?

12. This child killer and cannibal raised his large brood of children by himself after their mother passed away. They were appalled to hear of their father's crimes. Who was he?

13. This serial killer's moniker seems oddly suiting since his own death—or dirt nap—occurred in March 2020 while he awaited execution.

14. After hours of drinking and carousing, this serial killer broke into student housing and murdered all the young women there except one who was later able to identify him.

15. Which government agency is tasked with handling serial murder cases?

16. Is it true some states put a maximum dollar amount on the cost of a condemned prisoner's last meal?

17. If you answered "Yes," what do you think that dollar amount is?

18. Is it true a company called Last Meals Delivery offers a service in which you can receive an executed prisoner's last meal?

19. The last words of this serial killer were, *"Kiss my ass!"*

a. Carl Panzram

b. Charles Manson

c. Richard Ramirez

d. John Wayne Gacy

20. Which American state has produced the most serial killers?

21. True or False: Having been a manager at KFC in his younger days, John Wayne Gacy still loved the Colonel's chicken enough to request it as his last meal.

True

False

22. Sissy Spacek played a movie character loosely based on this serial killer:

a. Aileen Wuornos

b. Dorothea Puente

c. Carol Fugate

d. Rosemary West

23. This convicted killer was said to have turned his associates into "mindless robots" who killed at his bidding.

    a. Leonard Lake

    b. David Berkowitz

    c. Fred West

    d. Charles Manson

24. Which Manson Family member owned a wig shop in a trendy L.A. locale?

    a. Linda Kasabian

    b. Charles Manson

    c. Susan Atkins

    d. Charles "Tex" Watson

25. I confessed to over 90 murders. I could not remember the names of my victims, but I drew their portraits from memory to help police identify them. Who am I?

a. The Zodiac Killer

b. Doug Clark

c. Samuel Little

d. Paul John Knowles

26. Which American state has the most serial killers?

a. Rhode Island

b. California

c. Oklahoma

d. New Mexico

27. Which serial killer of boys and young men performed as Pogo the Clown at charitable events and children's parties?

a. Joel Rifkin

b. Ted Bundy

c. Arthur Shawcross

d. John Wayne Gacy

28. I enjoyed dressing in women's clothing, posing myself bound up, and taking photos. Who am I?

a. Rodney Alcala

b. William Bonin

c. Jeffrey Dahmer

d. Dennis Rader

29. Gary Gilmore was willing to donate his organs after execution but joked that this might be the only organ worth harvesting. What was it?

a. Eyes

b. Heart

c. Kidneys

d. Skin

30. In which month are most serial killers born?

   a. March

   b. November

   c. July

   d. December

31. This state is the only one to keep a record of condemned prisoners' last words:

   a. South Carolina

   b. Oklahoma

   c. California

d. Utah

32. I used to love babysitting, and the neighborhood kids loved me too. Who am I?

a. Ed Gein

b. Aileen Wuornos

c. Charles Manson

d. Karla Homolka

33. Who was the prosecutor in the Manson trial?

a. Alan Dershowitz

b. Bob Egan

c. Marcia Clark

d. Vincent Bugliosi

34. In what year was the "Jack the Ripper" case file closed?

   a. It is still open

   b. 1892

   c. 2018

   d. 1988

---

35. True or False: Most serial killers are social outsiders who keep to themselves.

   True

   False

---

36. Which of the following was *not* a California serial killer?

   a. Andrew Cunanan

   b. Doug Clark

   c. Angelo Buono

d. Richard Ramirez

37. Until recently, being identified through DNA, this victim of Henry Lee Lucas was known only as:

a. Yellow Hat

b. Blue Shirt

c. Orange Socks

d. Green Sweater

38. *"For heavens [sic]*

Sake catch me

Before I kill more

I cannot control myself."

This message was found at a crime scene of which serial killer?

a. The Happy Face Killer

b. The Confession Killer

c. The Lipstick Killer

d. The Zodiac

39. In which state was Bundy executed?

    a. California

    b. Colorado

    c. Washington

    d. Florida

40. What moniker was given to Ed Gein?

    a. The Butcher of Plainfield

    b. The Wild Man of Wisconsin

    c. The Cowardly Killer

    d. The Mama's Boy Murderer

41. How many "official" victims are attributed to "Jack the Ripper"?

    a. 13

    b. 5

    c. 3

    d. 15

42. Which of the following Manson family members was not at the Cielo Drive murders?

    a. Charles "Tex" Watson

    b. Susan Atkins

    c. Patricia Krenwinkel

    d. Bobby Beausoleil

43. True or False: Keith Jesperson became known as the "Happy Face Killer" because he would always leave a sticky note with a smiley face drawn on it nearby.

True

False

44. What color was the house belonging to Paul Bernardo and Karla Homolka?

a. Pink

b. Black

c. Purple

d. Brown

45. What clothing item did Dennis Nilsen use to dispatch his victims?

a. Stockings

b. Scarf

c. Necktie

d. Socks

46. Who was the first victim of Paul Bernardo and Karla Homolka?

    a. Paul's Sister

    b. Karla's Best Friend

    c. Paul's Niece

    d. Karla's Sister

47. I fathered a baby while on Death Row. Who am I?

    a. Ted Bundy

    b. Richard Ramirez

    c. Charles Ng

    d. Fred West

48. True or False: Ted Bundy used only his suave manner to get young women into his car.

   True

   False

49. True or False: "The Toy Box Killer" was the real-life inspiration for the Saw movies.

   True

   False

50. True or False: Serial killers look just like the rest of us.

   True

   False

IV

Trivia Answer Sheet

1. D.

2. D. This excerpt is from Jack the Ripper's "From Hell" letter.

3. B.

4. True.

5. C. Albert Fish was, in actuality, executed.

6. D.

7. D.

8. True.

9.   David Berkowitz.

10. Herb Baumeister.

BONUS: Baumeister's home was Fox Hollow Farms.

11. Carol Bundy.

12. Albert Fish.

13. The Grim Sleeper, Lonnie Franklin, Jr.

14. Richard Speck.

15. The FBI.

16. True.

17. In Florida, the limit is $40.

18. True.

19. D.

20. New York leads the U.S. in serial murders.

21. True.

22. C.

23. D.

24. D. Charles "Tex" Watson ran a popular wig shop during his time in L.A.

25. C.

26. B.

27. D.

28. D.

29. A.

30. B.

31. C.

32. A.

33. D. Bugliosi also authored the most famous book about the Manson murders, *Helter Skelter*.

34. B.

35. False. Many serial killers have a talent for decompartmentalizing and otherwise putting on the "mask of

sanity," making social relationships relatively easy for them to maintain.

36. A.

37. C. "Orange Socks" was identified as Debra Jackson.

38. C.

39. D.

40. A.

41. B.

42. D. Bobby Beausoleil was in prison at the time of the murders.

43. False. The smiley face appeared on letters sent to the media.

44. A.

45. C.

46. D.

47. A.

48. False. He also used a crowbar.

49. False.

50. True.

References

"Serial Killers: Evolution, Antisocial Personality Disorder, and Psychological Interventions," Beth I. Cook, 2011. https://alfredadler.edu/sites/default/files/Cook%20MP%202011.pdf

CBC Doc Zone, "The Psychopathy Checklist." www.cbc.ca, https://www.cbc.ca/doczone/features/the-hare-psychotherapy-checklist

Psychology Today: "Homicidal Triad: Predictor of Violence or Urban Myth?" www.psychologytoday.com, https://www.psychologytoday.com/us/blog/witness/201205/homicidal-triad-predictor-violence-or-urban-myth

Independent, "Three Types of Parents Most Likely to Raise a Murderer." http://www.independent.co.uk, https://www.independent.co.uk/life-style/health-and-families/mothers-three-types-murdererchild-son-daughter-uber-anti-passive-a7921551.html

Medical Xpress, "The Preferred Jobs of Serial Killers and Psychopaths." medicalxpress.com, https://medicalxpress.com/news/2018-05-jobs-serial-killers-psychopaths.html

Life Daily, "The 10 Worst Serial Killers of the 20th Century." www.lifedaily.com, http://www.lifedaily.com/the-10-worst-serial-killers-of-the-20th-century/

Crime Museum, "Serial Killer Victim Selection." www.crimemuseum.org, https://www.crimemuseum.org/crime-library/serial-killers/serial-killer-victim-selection/

Healthy Place, "Treatment for Psychopaths: Can the Psychopath Be Cured?" www.healthyplace.com https://www.healthyplace.com/personality-disorders/psychopath/treatment-for-psychopaths-can-the-psychopath-be-cured

"Psychopathology and the Ability to do Otherwise," Hanna Pickard. 1990. https://www.ncbi.nlm.nih.gov/pmc/articles/PMC4412198

ABC News, "Why Killers Cannibalize." abcnews.go.com, https://abcnews.go.com/US/story?id=90012&page=1

The Guardian, "What Makes a Serial Killer?" www.theguardian.com, https://www.theguardian.com/us-news/2018/aug/10/what-makes-a-serial-killer#maincontent

"Natural Born Celebrities: Serial Killers in American Culture," David Schmid. https://www.press.uchicago.edu/Misc/Chicago/738671.html

Crime Capsule, "Which State Has Produced the Most Serial Killers?" crimecapsule.com, https://crimecapsule.com/which-state-has-produced-the-most-serial-killers/

How Not to be a Victim, Dr. Maurice Godwin. http://www.drmauricegodwin.com/hownottobeavictim.html

The Unz Review, "The Decline in Serial Killers." www.unz.com, https://www.unz.com/isteve/the-decline-in-serial-killers

Murderpedia, "Bruce George Lee." murderpedia.org, http://murderpedia.org/male.L/l/lee-bruce-george.ht

Edmund Kemper Stories: www.edmundkemperstories.com,

Deseret News, "Executor Was Chosen From a List of Applicants." www.deseret.com, https://www.deseret.com/1989/1/25/18792770/executioner-was-chosen-from-a-list-ofapplicants

Psychology Today, "Serial Killer Ghosts." www.psychologytoday.com, https://www.psychologytoday.com/us/blog/shadow-boxing/201510/serial-killer-ghosts

Psychology Today, "Killer's Remorse." www.psychologytoday.com, https://www.psychologytoday.com/us/blog/shadow-boxing/201704/killers-remorse

Business Insider, "The Sinister Story of Nike's 'Just Do It' Slogan." www.businessinsider.com, https://www.businessinsider.com/nike-just-do-it-inspired-utah-killer-gary-gilmore-2019-7

Ranker, "20 Serial Killers Who Served in the Military." m.ranker.com, https://m.ranker.com/list/22-serial-killers-who-served-in-the-military/ranker-crime

Providence Journal, "Craig Price Gets 25 Years in Stabbing of Inmate." www.providencejournal.com https://www.providencejournal.com/news/20190118/craig-price-gets-25-years-in-stabbing-of-inmate

Ecperez, "Las Poquianchis: The Macabre Case That Shocked Mexico." ecperez.blogspot.com, http://ecperez.blogspot.com/2009/10/las-poquianchis-macabre-case-that.html

Daily Perversion, "Has Anyone Ever Survived the Electric Chair?" dailyperversion.blogspot.com, http://dailyperversion.blogspot.com/2011/07/has-anyone-ever-survived-electric-chair.html

True Crime Magazine, "6 Most Evil Serial Killers Brutally Murdered in Prison." www.thecrimemag.com https://www.thecrimemag.com/6-evil-serial-killers-brutally-murdered-prison/

Fact Republic, "50 Creepy and Unsettling Facts About Serial Killers." factrepublic.com, https://factrepublic.com/50-creepy-and-unsettling-facts-about-serial-killer

The Line Up, "Wayne Nance: The Suspected Serial Killer Who Was Never Found Guilty." the-line-up.com, https://the-line-up.com/wayne-nance-the-suspected-serial-killer-who-was-never-found-guilty

Listverse, "10 Kidnapped Children Who Escaped Death." listverse.com, https://listverse.com/2012/11/02/10-kidnapped-children-found-alive/

Medium, "Meet the Serial Killer Whisperer." gen.medium.com, https://gen.medium.com/meet-the-serial-killer-whisperer-dccd0a6c6b9b

CBS News, "Illinois' First Posthumous Clemency Granted to Man Who Died Behind Bars." www.cbsnews.com, https://www.cbsnews.com/news/grover-thompson-illinois-1st-posthumous-clemency-granted-to-man-who-died-behind-bars/

Eat & Drink, "Dining With the Dead: Last Meals Delivery Service." www.blogto.com, https://www.blogto.com/eat_drink/2008/09/dining_with_the_dea d_last_meals_delivery_service

The Vidocq Society: https://www.vidocq.org/

"The Macdonald Triad: Predictor of Violence or Urban Myth?" Kori Ryan. 2017. https://www.researchgate.net/profile/Kori_Ryan/publication/4523 9462_The_Macdonald_triad_predictor_of_violence_or_urban_my th_by_Kori_Ryan/links/5961c6170f7e9b819460d535

Serial Killer Information Database, Radford University: http://maamodt.asp.radford.edu/Serial%20Killer%20Information %20Center/Project%20Description.htm

FBI: https://www.fbi.gov/

Berry, Brian. *SERIAL KILLERS: 130 Facts and Trivia.* 2019. Independently Published.

Lequip, Gary. *50 Serial Killers: Bloody Protagonists of History's Worst Murder Sprees.* 2015. Cooltura.

Veysey, Nancy Alyssa. *Paul Bernardo and Karla Homolka: The Horrific True Story Behind Canada's Ken and Barbie Killers.* 2018. Sea Vision Publishing. New York.

Veysey, Kurtis-Giles. *Murderous Minds Volume 3: Stories of Real Life Murderers That Escaped the Headlines.* 2018. Sea Vision Publishing. New York.

Encyclopedia Britannica, "Ned Kelly: Australian Bandit." www.britannica.com, https://www.britannica.com/biography/Ned-Kelly-Australian-bandit

Casebook: Jack the Ripper, "Suspects: Dr. Thomas Neil Cream." casebook.org, https://casebook.org/suspects/cream.html

Executed Today, "1892, Thomas Neill Cream." www.executedtoday.com, http://www.executedtoday.com/2017/11/15/1892-thomas-neill-cream-i-am-jack-the/

Murderpedia, "Robert William Pickton." Murderpedia.org http://murderpedia.org/male.P/p/pickton-robert.htm

HPR, "Eugene Butler Had a Secret." hpr1.com, https://hpr1.com/index.php/feature/culture/eugene-butler-had-a-secret-niagaras-unsolved-murder-mystery/

People Pill, "Lyda Southard." peoplepill.com, https://peoplepill.com/people/lyda-southard/

The Washington Post, "He's Good-Looking, But the Devil's Good-Looking, Too." www.washingtonpost.com, https://www.washingtonpost.com/news/morning-mix/wp/2018/05/08/hes-good-looking-but-the-devils-good-looking-too-ohio-serial-killer-shawn-grate-convicted-of-murder/

Murderpedia, "Joseph Edward Duncan." murderpedia.org, http://murderpedia.org/male.D/d/duncan-joseph-edward.htm

Murderpedia, "David Parker Ray." murderpedia.org,
    http://murderpedia.org/male.R/r/ray-david-parker.htm

WickedWe, "Kenneth McDuff." wickedwe.com,
    https://wickedwe.com/kenneth-mcduff/

The Lineup, "Death in the Heartland." the-line-up.com, https://the-line-up.com/charles-starkweather-caril-ann-fugate

Biography, "Ariel Castro." www.biography.com,
    https://www.biography.com/crime-figure/ariel-castro

Murder By Gaslight, "The Legend of Lavinia Fisher."
    www.murderbygaslight.com,
    http://www.murderbygaslight.com/2010/10/legend-of-lavinia-fisher.html

Murderpedia, "Judias Anna Buenoano." murderpedia.org
    https://murderpedia.org/female.B/b/buenoano-judy.htm

ThoughtCo. "Profile of Serial Killer Debra Brown." www.thoughtco.com,
    https://www.thoughtco.com/serial-killer-debra-brown-973117

NWI Times, "True Crime: The Murder Spree of Alton Coleman and Debra
    Brown." www.nwitimes.com,
    https://www.nwitimes.com/news/state-and-regional/true-crime-the-murder-spree-of-alton-coleman-and-debra-brown/article_05b1a602-dd94-5e53-8f4e-345681725c4d.html

Murderpedia, "Sharon Kinne." murderpedia.org,
    https://murderpedia.org/female.K/k/kinne-sharon.htm

Murderpedia, "Juana Barraza." murderpedia.org,
    http://www.murderpedia.org/female.B/b/barraza-juana.htm

Murderpedia, "Rosemary West." murderpedia.org,
    http://www.murderpedia.org/female.W/w/west-rosemary.htm

All That's Interesting, "The Monstrous Crimes of The Dorothea Puente." allthatsinteresting.com, https://allthatsinteresting.com/dorothea-puente

Crime Museum, "Dorothea Puente." www.crimemuseum.org, https://www.crimemuseum.org/crime-library/serial-killers/dorothea-puente/

Murderpedia, "Nannie Doss." murderpedia.org, http://murderpedia.org/female.D/d/doss-nannie.htm

Schechter, Harold. *Fatal.* 2003. Pocket Books. New York.

All That's Interesting, "The Unsolved Mystery of the Redhead Murders." allthatsinteresting.com, https://allthatsinteresting.com/redhead-murders

FBI, "Serial Murder: Pathways for Investigations." www.fbi.gov, https://www.fbi.gov/file-repository/serialmurder-pathwaysforinvestigations.pdf/view

AJC, "Who are Georgia's Most Notorious Serial Killers?" www.ajc.com, https://www.ajc.com/news/crime--law/who-are-georgia-most-notorious-serial-killers/3inDJTGdZ4NOWnu2mWjswM/

WickedWe, "Cary Stayner." wickedwe.com, https://wickedwe.com/cary-stayner/

The Ghost in my Machine, "Unresolved: The Redhead Murders." theghostinmymachine.com, https://theghostinmymachine.com/2018/08/27/unresolved-redhead-murders-bible-belt-strangler-inexact-art-identifying-serial-murder/

FBI, "2018 Crime in the United States." ucr.fbi.gov, https://ucr.fbi.gov/crime-in-the-u.s/2018/crime-in-the-u.s.-2018/tables/expanded-homicide-data-table-8.xls

AZ Cential, "Aaron Saucedo Officially Charged in 'Serial Street Shooter' Murders." www.azcentral.com, https://www.azcentral.com/story/news/local/phoenix-breaking/2017/06/30/aaron-saucedo-officially-charged-serial-street-shooter-murders/443027001/

Acknowledgements

This is a special thanks to the following readers who have taken time out of their busy schedule to be part of the True Crime Seven Team. Thank you all so much for all the feedback and support!

James, Patricia Oliver, Rebecca Donnell, Jo Donna Hoevet, Joan Baker, Bonnie Kernene, Marty Fox, Dezirae, Christy Riemenschneider, Valencia, Donna Reif, Marcie Walters, Kathy Morgan, Rebecca Stallman Catazaro, Anna Mccown, Jason C. Tillery, Tina Shattuck, Lisa Marie Fraser, Penelope Bieniek, Lee Fowley, Sandy Van Domelen, Rebecca Ednie, Dallas Packer, Karen Harris, Paul Kelley, Jo-Lee Sears, Colleen, Lee Barta, Beth Alfred, Cindy Harcar, Judy Stephens, Susan M. Leedy, Jami Bridgman, Huw, Angie Grafton, Rachel B, Dannnii Desjarlais, Jeanie, Amanda, Irene Dobson, Annette Estrella, Remy Tankel-Carroll, Sherry Whitaker, Kelley Schroeder, Patricia Jeter, John Arvidsson, Anna, Tim Haight, Joy Page, Donna, Natalie Gwinn, Martyn Heaney, Tara Pendley, Libertysusan Gabor, Amanda Gallegos, John, Gordon Carmichael, James, Charles Junkin, Nick, Bessie, Damon Geddins, Toni Marie Rinella, Merja Mikkonen, Cheryl Posadas, Landa-Lou Goodridge, Wanda Jones, Barbara English, Carol Ryan, Fran Joyner, Shane Neely, Allyssa Howells, Jason Barnum, Kurt Brown, Connie White, Muhammad Nizam Bin Mohtar, Cindy Sirois, Teresa, Jason, Amanda, Jannis M. Fetter, Julie Descant, Christopher, Karin Dennis, Lynne Ridley, Sena Schneider, Melissa Swain, Jennifer Hanlon, Dani Bigner, Rita, Jennifer Lloyd, Kelly, Amy Steagall Johnson, Brandy Swartz, Monde Magolo, Anj Panes, Sandra Driskell, Marshall Bellitire, Amanda Kliebert, Ole Pedersen, Joyce Carroll, Dee Simmons, Alexis Osborne, Kristin Schroeder, Michelle Babb, Kim Thurston, Shakila "Kiki" Robinson, Laurel Von Dobschutz, Sue Wells, Larry J. Field, Linda Blackburn, Cory Lindsey, Deborah Sparagna, Michelle Lee, Cathy Russell, Sharee Steffens, David Richardson, April Clarke, Sue Wallace, Stefanie Valentine, Tammy Sittlinger, Chris Hurte, Felix Sacco, James Valentine, Mark Sawyer, Thomas Stewart Rae, Kathleen Tardi, Traci Spelts, Danny West, Deborah Hanson, Alan Kleynenberg, Tamela L. Matuska, Michael Rilley, Sherry Sundin, Stefanie Mathis, Chad Mellor, Monica Bleen, Susan Weaver, Monica Yokel, Linda Shoemaker, Connie Lynn Music, Tina

Rattray-Green, Susan Ault, Janine, Samantha Watt, Shelia Clark, Michele Gosselin, Tanya Jack, Karen Smith, Alicia Gir, Casey Renee Bates, Shannon Fiene, Cara Butcher, Janet Kazimi, Rebecca Roberts, Jennifer Jones, Leigh Lombardi, Adrian Brown, Marcia Heacock, Lisa Slat, Amy Hart, Richard Allen, Deirdre Green, Janet Elam, Paula Lookabill, Bambi Dawn Goggio, Diane Kourajian, Rebecca Mullis, Abriel Miller, Jamie Dome, Tammy, Jon Wiederhorn, Linda J Evans, Diane Kremski, Tina Bullard, Debbie Cochran, Crystal Clark, Jamie Rasmussen, Rebecca Adams, Myene Kelley, Doreen Marrisett, Melody Sanderson, Awilda Roman, Corey Lea Simpson, Don Price, Patricia Fulton, Eoin Corr, Cindy Selby, Amy Edwards, Debbie Hill, Robyn Byers, Nancy Harrison, Leigh Morrow, Miranda Sowers, Matthew Lawson, Bill Willoughby, Joy Riester, Alex Slocomb, David Edmonds, Robert Shaw

Continue Your Exploration Into

The Murderous Minds

Excerpt From List of Twelve Collection 1

I

Marjorie Orbin

"What this seems to be is a revelation of your very darkest side, ma'am," said Judge Arthur Anderson, as he stared at Marjorie Orbin during her sentencing hearing. "When that dark side is unleashed, it's about as dark as it gets," he continued.

The judge spoke these words from his bench on September 8th, 2004, in a courtroom in Phoenix, Arizona. It was the start of fall in Arizona, a welcome reprieve from the blistering heat of the summer. It was not only the torrid heat that ended, however, but a dark chapter of this desert community's crime annals.

A Grisly Find

The residents of Phoenix enjoy a patchwork of preserved desert areas throughout the city. However, on October 23rd, 2004, the rugged beauty of the area was eclipsed by a morbid find at the corner of Tatum and Dynamite Road, in North Phoenix. The Phoenix Police Department's 911 call center received a panicked call from an individual who was hiking in the area.

Police quickly arrived at the desert location, and the hiker led them to a spot that was not far off from the residential streets that surrounded the reservation. When the officers reached the site, they instantly knew that this was not a routine call. Detective Dave Barnes, of the Missing Persons Unit, arrived on the scene minutes later. A putrid smell filled the air as Barnes walked toward a 50-gallon Rubbermaid bin. "As we walked up, you could smell death in the air. Once you smell it, you know what it is for the rest of your life...it's the first time I had ever seen anything like that, where it's – just a piece of body," he would later say.

Barnes removed the lid and carefully opened the black trash bag contained within. Inside the trash bag was the bloody, dismembered torso of an adult male. Barnes would later tell a reporter, "All of the insides, all of the internal organs, intestines were missing...I thought, 'Who could do this to a human being? Cut off his arms, his legs, his head?'"

The grisly find was located less than two miles from the home of Marjorie Orbin, who lived in the 17000 Block of North 55th Street. Butcher had a strong suspicion that he had just found the torso of her missing husband; Marjorie had filed a missing person's report on September 22nd, 2004.

Jay Orbin was the successful owner of Jayhawk International, a dealership that specialized in Native American Art. He frequently traveled for business purposes, and it was not unusual for him to be gone three weeks out of the month. It was through his business travels that Jay met Marjorie.

The Stripper And The Salesman

Marjorie had been married seven times before meeting Jay at the age of 35. Marjorie was unable to conceive children and had lived a life with herself as the central focus. She entered each relationship looking for her Prince Charming, but it never happened.

Michael J. Peter was a very successful businessman who had made millions creating upscale strip clubs around the world. Marjorie left Peter because she believed he was cheating on her.

She moved to Las Vegas, where she danced at a strip club. It was at this strip club in 1993 that she met Jay, who was traveling through Las Vegas. They had been dating for a while when Jay proposed to Marjorie, offering to pay for fertility treatments if she married him. Marjorie accepted Jay's proposal, and they got married at the Little White Wedding Chapel in Las Vegas.

Soon afterward, they moved to Phoenix, where Jay lived. Marjorie was able to conceive and gave birth to their son, Noah. The couple divorced in 1997 but continued to live together. Marjorie had problems with the IRS and did not want Jay's assets to be vulnerable.

Jay's Disappearance

September 8th, 2004, Jay was driving back to Phoenix from a business meeting when he got a call from his mother, wishing him a happy birthday. That call was the last time anyone spoke to Jay.

When Jay's parents, brothers, and friends called his home, Marjorie told them that he had gone on a business trip and would not be returning until September 20th. During that time, those who cared about Jay could not reach him on his cell phone. His parents and friends expressed their concern to Marjorie; however, she said she did not know what was going on with him.

People who spoke to Marjorie about Jay stated that she expressed little concern for his welfare. Jay's intended return date passed, and still, nobody could reach him. When they inquired with Marjorie, she continued to remain aloof to their concerns. After continued pressure from friends and family, a missing person's report was filed on September 22nd.

Suspicion Is Raised

The Police Department assigned Detective Jan Butcher to the case. She interviewed Marjorie, who indicated that the last time she'd seen Jay was on August 28th, when he had attended his son's birthday. Butcher became suspicious of Marjorie on September 28th, after leaving voicemail messages for her before she called back. "I asked her to provide me the license plate of the vehicle Jay was driving. She said she would call me back. She never did. So, that was a little bit odd," she later told a reporter.

From that point on, Butcher's suspicions only continued to grow. Credit card and phone tower records indicated that Jay had arrived at his home in Phoenix on September 28th, which didn't match Marjorie's claim that she had last seen him on August 28th.

When detectives checked Jay's credit card records, they found that Marjorie was spending thousands of dollars, including purchasing a $12,000 baby grand piano, while the business account had a withdrawal of $45,000. Within one day of reporting Jay missing, she had liquidated a total of $100,000 from Jay's personal and business accounts.

A final cause for suspicion arose during a call that Detective Butcher made to Marjorie requesting that she take a polygraph test. Butcher heard Marjorie remark to someone in the background, "You know what? She wants me to take a polygraph tomorrow." A male voice replied, "You tell her to go f--- herself."

Butcher obtained a search warrant and went to Marjorie's home, accompanied by a SWAT team. The SWAT team forced their way in and encountered an adult male, Larry Weisberg. Larry was Marjorie's new boyfriend and the voice that had been heard in the background of the phone call. Weisberg was combative, resulting in police tasing him.

Police searched the premises and found a large number of credit cards belonging to Jay, plus his business checkbook, items that he always kept with him when traveling. Though police did not make any arrests, their surveillance of Marjorie deepened. It was shortly after Marjorie's home was searched that police found Jay's torso in the Rubbermaid bin in the desert.

DNA evidence confirmed the torso belonged to Jay Orbin. The Maricopa County Medical Examiner's Office inspected the torso and concluded Jay had been shot and his body frozen. At some point, the body had been defrosted, and a jigsaw was used to dismember and decapitate it.

When searching Jay's business, police found a packet of jigsaw blades, with some of the blades missing. The Medical Examiner's Office determined the blades from the business matched the cut marks on the torso, where the limbs and vertebrae were severed.

Detectives traced the UPC code on the Rubbermaid bin back to a Lowes Home Improvement store in Scottsdale. The detectives scored big when they viewed video from the store's surveillance cameras and saw Marjorie purchasing the Rubbermaid bin, trash bags, and black tape. Police detained Marjorie when they caught her forging Jay's signature while making a purchase at a Circuit City store.

Jay's remaining body parts were never found, nor the gun that was used to shoot Jay.

Marjorie and her boyfriend, Larry Weisberg, were arrested on December 6, 2004. Weisberg was offered immunity if he agreed to testify against Marjorie, who was sentenced to life in prison on October 1st, 2009.

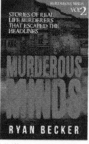
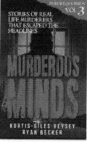
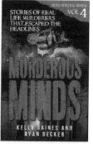

About True Crime Seven

True Crime Seven Books is about exploring the stories behind all the murderous minds in the world. From unknown murderers to infamous serial killers. It is our goal to create content that satisfies true crime enthusiasts' morbid curiosities while sparking new ones.

Our writers come from all walks of life but with one thing in common, and that is they are all true crime enthusiasts. You can learn more about them below:

Ryan Becker is a True Crime author who started his writing journey in late 2016. Like most of you, he loves to explore the process of how individuals turn their darkest fantasies into a reality. Ryan has always had a passion for storytelling. So, writing is the best output for him to combine his fascination with psychology and true crime. It is Ryan's goal for his readers to experience the full immersion with the dark reality of the world, just like how he used to in his younger days.

Nancy Alyssa Veysey is a writer and author of true crime books, including the bestselling *Mary Flora Bell: The Horrific True Story Behind an Innocent Girl Serial Killer*. Her medical degree and work in the field of forensic psychology, along with postgraduate studies in criminal justice, criminology, and pre-law, allow her to bring a unique perspective to her writing.

Kurtis-Giles Veysey is a young writer who began his writing career in the fantasy genre. In late 2018, he parlayed his love and knowledge of history into writing nonfiction accounts of true crime stories that occurred in centuries past. Told from a historical perspective, Kurtis-Giles brings these victims and their killers back to life with vivid descriptions of these heinous crimes.

Kelly Gaines is a writer from Philadelphia. Her passion for storytelling began in childhood and carried into her college career. She received a B.A. in English from Saint Joseph's University in 2016, with a concentration in Writing Studies. Now part of the real world, Kelly enjoys comic books, history documentaries, and a good scary story. In her true-crime work, Kelly focuses on the motivations of the killers and backgrounds of the victims to draw a complete picture of each individual. She deeply enjoys writing for True Crime Seven and looks forward to bringing more spine-tingling tales to readers.

James Parker, the pen-name of a young writer from New Jersey, who started his writing journey with play-writing. He has always been fascinated with the psychology of murderers and how the media might play a role in their creation. James loves to constantly test out new styles and ideas in his writing, so one day, he can find something cool and unique to himself.

Brenda Brown is a writer and an illustrator-cartoonist. Her art can be found in books distributed both nationally and internationally. She has also written many books related to her graduate degree in psychology and her minor in history. Like many true crime enthusiasts, she loves exploring the minds of those who see the world as a playground for expressing the darker side of themselves—the side that people usually locked up and hid from scrutiny.

Genoveva Ortiz is a Los Angeles-based writer who began her career writing scary stories while still in college. After receiving a B.A. in English in 2018, she shifted her focus to nonfiction and the real-life horrors of crime and unsolved mysteries. Together with True Crime Seven, she is excited to further explore the world of true crime through a social justice perspective.

You can learn more about us and our writers at

https://truecrimeseven.com/about/

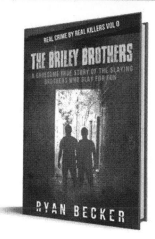

Dark Fantasies Turned Reality

Prepare yourself, we're not going to **hold back on details or cut out any of the gruesome truths...**

Printed in Great Britain
by Amazon